Young Person's Occupational Outlook Handbook

Second Edition

Based on information from the U.S. Department of Labor

JIST Works, Inc.

Young Person's Occupational Outlook Handbook, Second Edition

Published by JIST Works, Inc.
720 North Park Avenue
Indianapolis, IN 46202-3490
Phone: 317-264-3720   Fax: 317-264-3709
E-mail: jistworks@aol.com
Visit our Web site for information on other JIST products: http://www.jist.com

Editor: Sherri W. Emmons
Cover Design: Aleata Howard
Interior Design: Lynda Preston, Rockabye Design Production
Illustrator: Richard Scott Morris
Proofreader: Maureen McCrae-Shepley

Printed in the United States of America

02 01 00 99   9 8 7 6 5 4 3 2 1

We have been careful to provide accurate information throughout this book, but it is possible that errors and omissions have been introduced. Please consider this in making any career plans or other important decisions. Trust your own judgment above all else and in all things.

ISBN 1-56370-519-2

About This Book

This book presents information on about 250 major jobs. These jobs cover more than 85 percent of the workforce, and you are very likely to work in one or more of them during your life.

In looking over these jobs, we suggest that you consider every one that interests you. Remember that you are exploring job possibilities. The information will help you learn which classes to take and what additional training or education you will need to do that job. If a job requires more training or education than you think you can get, consider it anyway. There are many ways to finance an education, so don't eliminate any job possibility too soon.

The introduction will give you useful information to understand and use the book for career exploration. We hope this book will help you identify some new jobs to think about and some new possibilities to consider.

Table of Contents

Executive, Administrative, & Managerial Occupations

Professional & Technical Occupations

Marketing & Sales Occupations

Administrative Support, Including Clerical Occupations

Service Occupations

Mechanic, Installer, & Repairer Occupations

Construction Trades Occupations

Factory & Production Occupations

Introduction

This book was designed to help you explore a wide variety of jobs. This is important because your career decision is one of the most important decisions you will make in life. This book includes descriptions for 247 major jobs. These jobs together employ more than 85 percent of the American workforce. The job descriptions will answer questions like these:

* What do people in this job do all day?
* What training or education will I need to do the job?
* How much does the job pay?
* Will the job be in demand in the future?

The information in this book is based on another book titled the *Occupational Outlook Handbook* (the *OOH*). The *OOH* is published by the U.S. Department of Labor and is the most widely used source of career information available. Like the *OOH,* the *Young Person's Occupational Outlook Handbook* groups similar jobs together. This makes it easy to explore related jobs you might not know about. The job descriptions in the *OOH* are more detailed, and you can refer to it for more information on jobs that interest you.

Tips to Identify Jobs That Interest You

The table of contents lists all the jobs in this book, arranged into groups of similar jobs. Look through the list and choose one or more of the job groups that sound most interesting to you. Make a list of the jobs that interest you, then read the descriptions for those jobs.

The Information in Each Job Description

Each job description in this book uses the same format. They all include eight sections:

On the Job: This section has a short description of the duties and working conditions for the job.

Subjects to Study: Here you'll find some high school courses that will help you prepare for the job.

Discover More: This section has an activity you can do to learn more about the job, or a place to go for more information.

Related Jobs: This lists similar jobs you can consider.

Something Extra: These boxes have interesting, fun facts or stories related to the job.

 Education & Training: This tells you the education and training levels most employers expect for someone starting out in the job. Almost all jobs now require a high school diploma, so we do not include "high school graduate" as an option. Instead, we list the additional training or education the average high school graduate needs to get the job.

Here are the levels of training and education we've used:

Short-term OJT	=	On-the-job training that lasts up to six months.
Long-term OJT	=	On-the-job training that lasts up to two or more years.
Work experience	=	Work experience in a related job.
Voc/tech training	=	Formal vocational or technical training received in a school, apprenticeship, or cooperative education program or in the military. This training can last from a few months to two or more years and may combine classroom training with on-the-job experience.
Associate degree	=	A two-year college degree.
Bachelor's degree	=	A four-year college degree.
Master's degree	=	A bachelor's degree plus one or two years of additional education.
Doctoral degree	=	A master's degree plus two or more years of additional education.
Professional degree	=	Typically, a bachelor's degree plus two or more years of specialized education (for example, attorney, physician, and veterinarian).
Plus sign (+)	=	The plus sign indicates you need work experience in a related job as well as formal education. For example "Bachelor's degree +" means you need a bachelor's degree plus work experience in a related job.

Earnings: Dollar signs represent the approximate range of average earnings for a job.

$ = $15,000 or less per year

$$ = $15,001 to $23,000 per year

$$$ = $23,001 to $28,000 per year

$$$$ = $28,001 to $50,000 per year

$$$$$ = $50,001 or more per year

Job Outlook: This tells you if the job is likely to employ more or fewer people in the future.

Declining = Employment is expected to decrease by 5% or more.

Little change to some decline = Employment is expected to remain about the same or decrease as much as 5%.

Little change = Employment is expected to remain about the same.

Little change to some increase = Employment opportunities are expected to remain about the same or increase by up to 10%.

Average increase = Employment is expected to increase from 10% to 16%.

Above-average increase = Employment is expected to increase from 17% to 24%.

Rapid increase = Employment is expected to increase by 25% or more.

Using the Earnings and Job Outlook Information

Are lower earnings "bad" and higher earnings "good"? Is rapid growth in a job better than slow growth or a decline?

Many people do not consider jobs if they have low earnings or are not projected to grow rapidly. But we think you should look at earnings and growth as just two of several measures when you consider your job options. Here is some advice in looking at these important measures.

Earnings Information

The average adult worker in the United States earns about $25,000 a year, and the average four-year college graduate earns about $10,000 more than that. There is a clear connection between earnings and education, and it goes like this: The more you learn, the more you are likely to earn. But information on earnings can be misleading. Some people earn much more than the average, even in "low-paying" jobs. For example, some waiters and waitresses earn more than $50,000 a year, although the average earnings for these jobs are much lower. And some high school graduates earn much more than the average for four-year college graduates.

Earnings also vary widely for similar jobs with different employers or in different parts of the country. Finally, young workers usually earn a lot less than the average, because they have less work experience than the average worker in the same job.

This book presents earnings information for the "average" person in the job. But you should remember that half of all people in any job earn more than average, and half earn less. So don't eliminate a job that interests you based only on its average pay.

Job Outlook Information

The U.S. Department of Labor, a part of the federal government, collects job information from all over the country. The department uses some of this information to guess which jobs are likely to grow and which will decline—and by how much. The most recent information projects job growth for the next 10 years. Some jobs will grow faster than average. Others will grow slower than average. What's more, some jobs are likely to employ fewer people in 10 years than they do now.

But, as with earnings, job growth should be only one of the things you consider in planning your career. For example, jobs that employ small numbers of people may have rapid growth, but they won't generate nearly as many new jobs as a slow-growing but large field like "cashier." Don't eliminate jobs that interest you simply because they are not growing quickly. Even jobs that are "declining" will have some new openings for talented people, because workers leave the field for retirement or other jobs.

Some Things to Consider

Choosing your career is one of the most important decisions of your life. By exploring career options now, you will be better prepared to make good decisions later. Here are some things you should consider:

Your Interests: Think about what interests you. Your hobbies, school subjects you like or do well in, sports and clubs, home and family chores, volunteer activities, and other things can be clues to possible careers. For example, if you are interested in music, you might think about a job in the music industry.

Your Values: It is important to look for a job that lets you do something you believe in. For example, if you want to help people, you will be happier in a job that allows you to do that. Or you may be able to find a hobby or volunteer job that lets you do this outside of your job. Either way, it's worth thinking about.

Education and Training: How much education or training are you willing to consider? Most of the better-paying jobs today require training or education beyond high school. And more and more jobs require computer skills, technical training, or other specialized skills. It's true, "the more you learn, the more you are likely to earn." So you might want to consider getting a four-year degree or technical training after high school. Either of these options can lead to jobs with high pay and good opportunities. For now, you should consider any job that interests you, even if you aren't sure whether you can afford the training or education required. If you really want to do something, you can find a way.

Earnings: What you earn at your job is important, because it defines what kind of lifestyle you can afford. Higher-paying jobs usually require higher levels of training or education, or higher levels of responsibility.

Working Conditions: Do you like to work in an office or outside? Would you rather work by yourself or as part of a group? Do you want to be in charge? What kinds of people would you like to work with? These are just some of the things to consider in planning your career.

Satisfaction: You will spend hundreds of hours working each year, and you will be happier if you are doing work you enjoy and are good at. Your interests and values can give you important clues to possible jobs.

Skills: What skills do you have? What skills do you need to get the jobs you want? What skills can you learn or improve with more training or education? The skills you have already, and the skills you can develop in the future, are important parts of making good career decisions.

Self-Employment: Did you know that more than 10 percent of all workers are self-employed or own their own businesses today? Head to the library and you'll find lots of books and other sources of information on this topic. If self-employment appeals to you, don't let anyone tell you "you're too young." Check it out!

Getting More Information

As you can see, there are a lot of things to consider in planning your career or job options. This book can help you find the jobs that interest you. But once you're done here, you'll want to get more information. Once you decide which jobs interest you, here are some places to learn more:

Check out the *Occupational Outlook Handbook*: The *OOH* has more thorough descriptions for each of the jobs in this book, so you should start there. It's available at your library. A book titled *America's Top 300 Jobs* includes all the *OOH* job descriptions, and you can order it through your local bookstore.

Visit the Library: You can find the *OOH* and many other career books, magazines, and other resources at most libraries. Ask your librarian for help in finding what you want.

Talk to People: Find people who work in jobs that interest you and "interview" them. Ask what they like and don't like about the job, how to get started, what education or training you need, and other details.

The Internet: If you have access to the Internet, you can find a lot of career information online.

Your Teacher: Ask your teacher for ideas on other sources of career information. He or she may be able to help you find more information in your school library or from other sources.

Remember, this book is only the beginning of your search for "the right career." Don't rule out any jobs because they seem out of reach or because they don't pay "enough." Follow your dreams, do your homework, and you'll figure out how to get from here to there.

Executive, Administrative, & Managerial Occupations

Accountants & Auditors

On the Job

Accountants and auditors prepare and check financial reports and taxes. They work for businesses and banks, the government, and individuals. Some are self-employed, working as consultants or preparing people's tax returns. Most use computers in their work.

Subjects to Study

Math, speech, business, economics, computer skills

Discover More

With your teacher's help, set up a banking system in your classroom. You can earn "class dollars" for good behavior, turning work in on time, and good attendance. You can spend those dollars on items from the "class store" or maybe on special privileges. Keep your bankbook up to date, recording each dollar you earn and each one you spend at the class store.

Related Jobs

Appraisers, loan officers, bank officers, actuaries, underwriters, tax collectors, and FBI special agents

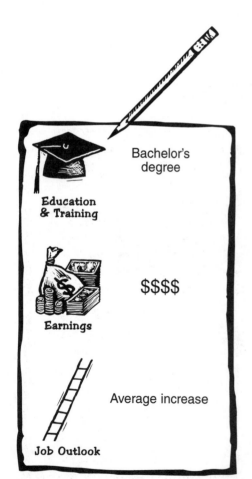

Education & Training
Bachelor's degree

Earnings
$$$$

Job Outlook
Average increase

Administrative Services Managers

On the Job

Administrative services managers work for large and small businesses and government agencies. They manage the services that keep businesses in business: the mailroom, food, security, parking, printing, purchasing, and payroll. In large companies, they may manage other workers. In small ones, they may be responsible for any or all of these services themselves.

Subjects to Study

English, math, speech, computer skills, business

Discover More

Divide your class into groups of four or five. Have each group take a turn planning a class activity. Groups will have to decide what supplies they need for their activity, who will bring them in, and how they will teach the activity. For example, you might teach your classmates to make paper fans or create an assembly line to produce birdhouses.

Related Jobs

Appraisers, buyers, clerical supervisors, cost estimators, property and real estate managers

Bachelor's degree +

Education & Training

$$$$

Earnings

Average increase

Job Outlook

Budget Analysts

Something Extra

A few years ago, newspapers across the country ran stories about the government buying $700 toilet seats. What was going on? The Defense Department had been buying items from the same companies for years, without checking to see if it was getting a fair price. Budget analysts were called in to clear up the mess, ensuring that your tax dollars won't be spent on overpriced toilet seats again.

On the Job

Budget analysts help businesses decide how much money they need to run, and how to spend that money. They check reports and accounts during the year to make sure the business is staying within its budget and making the best use of its assets. They also look for ways to save and use money more efficiently.

Subjects to Study

Math, business, economics, computer skills, statistics, accounting

Discover More

Imagine you are starting a business making widgets. Give yourself $10,000 to start, then decide how to spend the money. Do you need staff? How much will you pay them? What equipment and supplies do you need? Do you have to rent work space? Make a budget for your business. Can you make a profit?

Related Jobs

Accountants and auditors, economists, financial analysts, and loan officers

Education & Training
Bachelor's degree

Earnings
$$$$

Job Outlook
Average increase

Construction & Building Inspectors

On the Job

Construction and building inspectors make sure that the country's buildings, roads, sewers, dams, and bridges are safe. They may check electrical or plumbing systems, elevators, or the beams and girders on skyscrapers. They climb high ladders, crawl through underground tunnels, and squeeze into tight spaces to do their jobs.

Something Extra

In 1989, a magnitude 6.8 earthquake hit Armenia in Central Asia. Thousands of buildings collapsed, killing more than 25,000 people. A year later, San Francisco was hit with an even larger earthquake, yet only 62 people died.
Why the difference? Buildings, roads, and bridges in California must meet strict building codes. Those codes and the inspectors who enforce them saved thousands of lives.

Subjects to Study

Math, geometry, algebra, drafting, shop, computer skills

Discover More

Inspectors often use photographs in their reports. Practice your photography skills by taking pictures of building details in your neighborhood. Do you see anything that might be unsafe?

Related Jobs

Drafters, estimators, engineers, surveyors, architects, and construction managers

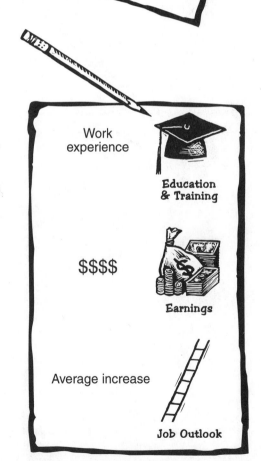

Work experience

Education & Training

$$$$

Earnings

Average increase

Job Outlook

Construction Managers

On the Job

Construction managers plan and direct construction projects. On small projects, they are responsible for all the people, materials, and equipment at a job site. They hire and schedule workers, make sure materials are delivered on time, and oversee the safety of the work site. They often work outdoors, and may be on call to deal with emergencies.

Subjects to Study

Math, shop, computer science, drafting, technology, business courses

Discover More

Taking shop courses at school, building small projects at home, and apprenticing with a skilled craft worker are some ways you can learn more about the construction industry.

Related Jobs

Architects, engineers, cost estimators, and landscape architects

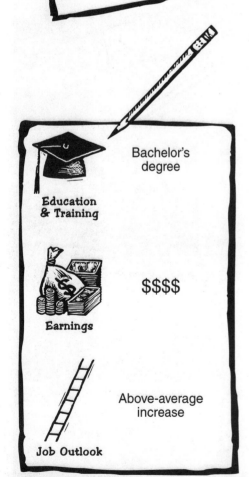

Education & Training
Bachelor's degree

Earnings
$$$$

Job Outlook
Above-average increase

Cost Estimators

On the Job

When a company is thinking about a new product, the owner needs to know how much it will cost to produce. What new machinery will be needed? How much will materials cost? How many workers will be hired? A cost estimator finds the least expensive way to make the best product. Cost estimators decide what supplies to use, find the best prices, estimate labor costs, and report back to the owner.

Something Extra

A cost estimator was called by a company to estimate the value of a load of scrap copper in the Mojave desert. The manager warned the estimator he might have trouble with the job. When the estimator arrived on site, he understood why. The company had been having such problems with thieves, it had dug a huge pit and put the copper inside. Then, for security, it had thrown in a bunch of rattlesnakes on top of the copper. The estimator peered into the pit, made his best guess, and high-tailed it home before he found out whose job it was to feed the snakes!

Subjects to Study

Math, computer science, technology programs, business, English, economics, statistics

Discover More

Plan a business making birdhouses from craft sticks. Decide how many you will make, then find the total cost of producing them. Include all your building materials (craft sticks, glue, and paint, for example), supplies (how about a hot glue gun?), and labor costs (what you pay your helpers). Call several stores to find the best prices. How much must you charge to make a profit?

Related Jobs

Appraisers, accountants, auditors, budget analysts, economists, loan officers, underwriters, and construction managers

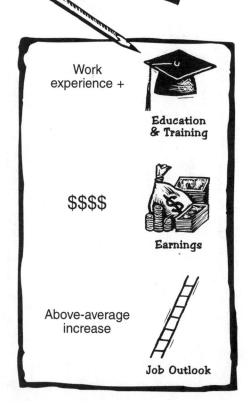

Work experience +

Education & Training

$$$$

Earnings

Above-average increase

Job Outlook

Education Administrators

On the Job

Education administrators are like the managers of schools, colleges, and universities. They develop programs, monitor students' progress, train teachers, and prepare budgets. They must communicate with parents, students, employers, and the community. They may be school principals, college presidents or deans, or school district superintendents.

Subjects to Study

English, speech, computer science, statistics, psychology, college prep courses

Discover More

Ask the principal or dean at your school if you can "apprentice" with him or her for a day or two, watching, asking questions, and helping out as needed. Does the workday end when school is out? Will you have to attend evening meetings? Are there aspects of the job you like or dislike?

Related Jobs

Health service administrators, social service agency administrators, recreation and park managers, museum directors, and library directors

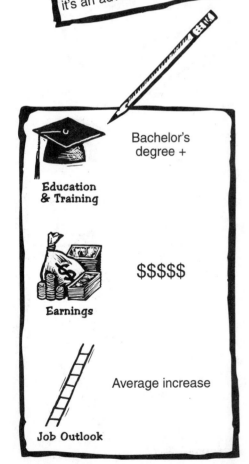

Education & Training — Bachelor's degree +

Earnings — $$$$$

Job Outlook — Average increase

Employment Interviewers

On the Job

Employment interviewers help people find jobs and employers find workers. In large companies, they interview people for job openings in different departments. At state employment offices, they match unemployed people with job openings in the community. At personnel or temporary employment agencies, they find workers for several different companies. They do background checks, assessments, and interviews to find the right person for the right job.

Something Extra

What do you think of when you hear the words head hunter? A warrior waving a spear and shrunken head in a late-night TV movie? Today's head hunters are employment interviewers. They spend their days recruiting lawyers, accountants, and computer scientists away from one company to work for another. Not as glamorous as the original image perhaps, but the pay is better!

Subjects to Study

English, speech, business, psychology, computer skills

Discover More

What do you want to do when you've graduated? (If you don't know, make something up!) Now interview for that job with a friend. Take turns being the employer and the job candidate. As the employer, ask your friend what skills he or she has to do the job. As the candidate, talk about your skills, interests, and education. Would you hire your friend? Would your friend hire you?

Related Jobs

Personnel officers, career counselors, community and vocational counselors, and salespeople

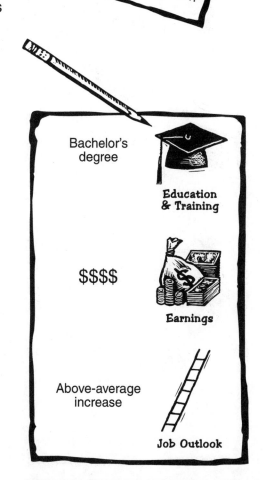

Bachelor's degree

Education & Training

$$$$

Earnings

Above-average increase

Job Outlook

Engineering, Science, & Computer Systems Managers

Something Extra

What do you think of when you hear the word *security*? An alarm, barred windows, maybe a guard?

In business today, the biggest security threat is often to the computers. American companies pay millions each year on network security, often paying computer scientists to "hack" their systems—that is, to try to break into the company's network, so the in-house team can see the system's weak points and correct them.

Education & Training
Bachelor's degree +

Earnings
$$$$$

Job Outlook
Rapid increase

On the Job

These workers plan and direct research, development, production, and computer-related activities. They hire engineers, scientists, and computer programmers. They manage and review the work in a business or lab and help determine salaries. They also decide what workers and equipment are needed to do certain jobs.

Subjects to Study

Math, physics, chemistry, shop and technology courses, computer skills, speech, business

Discover More

Take a tour of your school's computer lab. Does the lab instructor keep the computers in running order, or does the school use an outside contractor for that job? How often are the computers "defragged"? Are they checked regularly for viruses? These are just a few of the questions a computer systems manager must answer.

Related Jobs

Engineers, natural scientists, computer programmers, mathematicians, general managers, and top executives

Farmers & Farm Managers

On the Job

Because of the chemicals and equipment used, farming is a dangerous job. Farmers on crop farms work dawn to dusk through the growing season to produce the grains, fruits, and vegetables that feed the country. During the rest of the year, many work second jobs. On livestock farms, animals must be fed and watered every day, and dairy cows must be milked two or three times a day. Farmers must also have good business skills.

Something Extra

Say the word *farmer,* and most of us picture a man in overalls, riding a tractor or perhaps milking a cow. Some farmers, of course, do those things. But others hardly fit the standard image. Fish farmers in Georgia tend large lakes of small fish. Citrus farmers in Florida spend cold evenings covering tender trees with plastic to keep their fruits from freezing. Grape growers in the Napa Valley test their grapes for just the right sweetness before selling them to wine makers. There are as many kinds of farmers as there are products to eat!

Subjects to Study

Life sciences, mechanics and shop courses, math, business, computer skills, agriculture, physical education

Discover More

Planting, tending, and harvesting your own vegetable or flower garden is a good way to learn about crop farming. To learn more about animal farming, you could raise a small animal through the 4-H program in your community.

Related Jobs

Agricultural scientists, foresters and conservation scientists, landscape architects, and veterinary assistants

Long-term OJT to Bachelor's degree +

Education & Training

$$–$$$

Earnings

Little change to some decline

Job Outlook

Financial Managers

On the Job

Financial managers work for all kinds of businesses. Many work for banks, credit unions, or insurance companies. They prepare financial reports and make sure the business pays its taxes and has enough money to operate. They watch over the cash flow, manage the company's stocks, and communicate with investors. They also decide if the business needs to borrow money, lend money, or invest in stocks and bonds.

Subjects to Study

Math, English, business, accounting, writing and computer skills, speech, foreign languages

Discover More

Learn more about investing in the stock market by checking out these Web sites on the Internet:

The Young Investor
www.younginvestor.com

Kid's Money Web Resources
prodigy.com/kidsmoney/invlist.htm

Wall Street Report for Kids
www.geocities.com/WallStreet/3653

Related Jobs

Accountants and auditors, budget officers, credit analysts, loan officers, insurance consultants, real estate advisors, and underwriters

Education & Training
Bachelor's degree +

Earnings
$$$$$

Job Outlook
Above-average increase

Funeral Directors

On the Job

Funeral directors prepare bodies for burial or cremation. When someone dies, they help the family plan the funeral, prepare the obituary notice, and handle the paperwork. Most are licensed embalmers. Funeral directors are also business people: They prepare bills, keep financial records, and hire and manage a staff. Most work long, irregular hours.

Something Extra

More and more people are opting for cremation these days. And people sometimes choose unusual ways to deal with their ashes. "Star Trek" creator Gene Roddenberry's ashes were carried into space on the shuttle; 1960s rock icon Janis Joplin's were scattered off the California coast; and John Lennon's were wrapped as a Christmas gift and delivered to his wife, Yoko Ono.

Subjects to Study

Business, English, biology, chemistry, psychology, speech

Discover More

Take a class trip to a local funeral home. Ask the director about his or her job: Does the director do much counseling with grieving families? Does he or she also do embalming—preparing bodies for burial? Does the funeral home offer cremation services as well? Has the director had clients who have made unusual requests for their ashes?

Related Jobs

Clergy members, social workers, psychologists, psychiatrists, and health care professionals

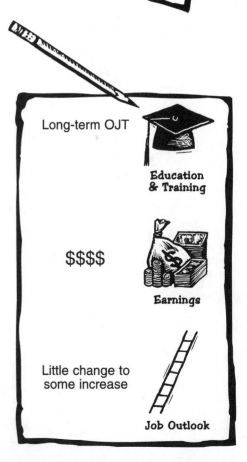

Long-term OJT

Education & Training

$$$$

Earnings

Little change to some increase

Job Outlook

General Managers & Top Executives

On the Job

General managers and top executives make policies and direct operations at businesses and government agencies. They decide a company's goals and make plans to meet them. They meet with other executives, boards of directors, government heads, and consultants to talk about things that could affect their business. They are responsible for the business's ultimate success or failure.

Subjects to Study

Math, English, business, accounting, speech, computer science, psychology

Discover More

You can learn more about being a leader by running for the student council at your school, taking a leadership position in a club or organization, or helping to plan activities at your school, church, or home.

Related Jobs

President, governors, mayors, commissioners, and legislators

Education & Training
Bachelor's degree +

Earnings
$$$$–$$$$$

Job Outlook
Above-average increase

Government Chief Executives & Legislators

On the Job

Government chief executives and legislators run cities, states, and the nation. Most are elected. Chief executives, such as the president or governor, oversee budgets, appoint department heads, and are responsible for how the government operates. Legislators pass or amend laws, approve budgets, and help resolve people's problems.

Something Extra

You might think being the governor, a senator, or even the president is a prestigious job, and you'd be right. Being a government chief executive definitely has its perks and privileges, including travel, good pay, public recognition, and a voice in what happens in our society.

But government executives must be as thick-skinned as an elephant in order to survive. They routinely see themselves ridiculed in magazines and newspapers and on TV talk shows.

Subjects to Study

English, speech, writing skills, psychology, government, history

Discover More

Run for a class or club office. Set some goals you would work for if you were elected. This will be your "platform." Enlist others to help with your campaign. Remember, your goals must be in line with those of the people who elect you. Your job is to serve them.

Related Jobs

Corporate chief executives and board members, and military generals

Bachelor's degree +

Education & Training

$$$$–$$$$$

Earnings

Little change

Job Outlook

Health Services Managers

On the Job

Health services managers plan, organize, and supervise the delivery of health care. They determine staffing and equipment needs and direct the public relations, marketing, and finances of hospitals, nursing homes, HMOs, clinics, and doctor's offices. They may be in charge of an entire organization or only one department within it.

Subjects to Study

Math, English, speech, writing skills, business, psychology, health

Discover More

To learn more about careers in the health-care field, try volunteering at a local nursing home or hospital in your community. Many have volunteers who read to or visit with patients and make small deliveries.

Related Jobs

Public health directors and underwriters

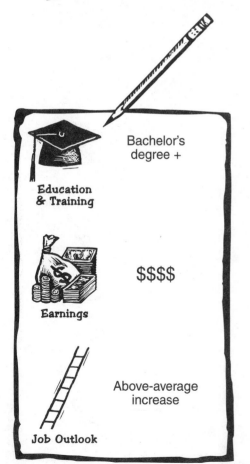

Education & Training
Bachelor's degree +

Earnings
$$$$

Job Outlook
Above-average increase

Hotel Managers & Assistants

On the Job

Hotel managers and assistants hire, train, and supervise the people who work in hotels and motels. They set room rates, handle billing, order food and supplies, and oversee the day-to-day operations of the hotel. Managers who work for hotel chains may organize and staff a new hotel, refurbish an older one, or reorganize one that is not operating well. Most work more than 40 hours a week, often at night and on weekends.

Something Extra

A lost child, missing luggage, mixed up reservations, a room that's too warm, a room that's too cold—hotel managers deal with these kinds of things on a daily basis. If something is wrong with the accommodations, hotel guests complain to the manager. These managers must be diplomats, problem-solvers, negotiators, and sometimes baby-sitters, too!

Subjects to Study

English, foreign languages, business, math, accounting, computer skills

Discover More

Call a local hotel and ask if you can "shadow" the front desk manager for a day. Ask about job responsibilities. What kinds of hours are required? How does the manager handle unpleasant customers? What emergencies has he or she faced in the last year?

Related Jobs

Restaurant managers, apartment building managers, retail store managers, and office managers

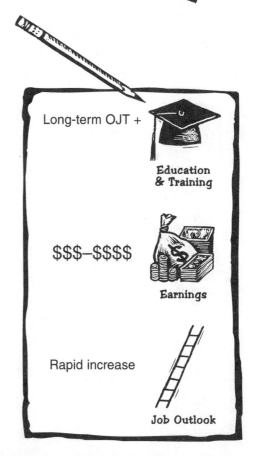

Long-term OJT +

Education & Training

$$$–$$$$

Earnings

Rapid increase

Job Outlook

Human Resources Specialists & Managers

On the Job

These workers find the best employees they can and match them with jobs in their company. They interview job candidates and train new workers. They may travel to college campuses to find the best job applicants. They also help to resolve conflicts among workers or between workers and management.

Subjects to Study

English, business, psychology, sociology, communications, writing skills, computer skills, foreign languages

Discover More

If your school has a conflict resolution team, volunteer to participate. If it does not, set up a team in your classroom. The team's job is to help out when two students are involved in a dispute. Team members hear both sides and come up with a fair solution. They may also teach conflict resolution skills to other students.

Related Jobs

Counselors, employment counselors, lawyers, psychologists, sociologists, social workers, public relations specialists, and teachers

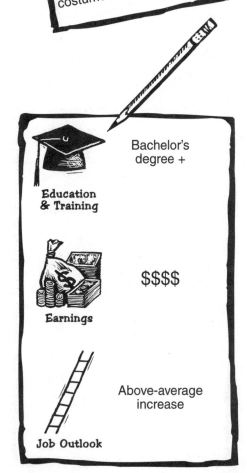

Education & Training
Bachelor's degree +

Earnings
$$$$

Job Outlook
Above-average increase

Industrial Production Managers

On the Job

These workers direct scheduling, staffing, equipment, quality control, and inventory in factories. Their main job is to get goods produced on time and within budget. They decide what equipment and workers to use and in what order. They also monitor the production run to make sure it stays on schedule and to fix any problems that arise.

Subjects to Study

Math, English, shop and technology courses, computer skills, business

Discover More

Plan an assembly-line process for making a craft. How many workers do you need? What materials and equipment will you use? How long will it take to make the item? How much will it cost? These are the questions a manager must answer.

Related Jobs

Operations managers, purchasing managers, traffic managers, sales engineers, manufacturer's sales representatives, and industrial engineers

Something Extra

You have to have 10,000 widgets ready by next Tuesday. Your widget painter cannot run at the same time as your widget packer. Your widget tops are arriving tomorrow, but the bottoms won't be in until the next day. On top of that, your widget-assembling workers charge double time if they have to work nights. You must decide the best way to run the assembly line and when to run each machine. You also have to decide whether to have your workers on overtime, or hire temporary helpers. And you must decide it all by noon. You're a production manager!

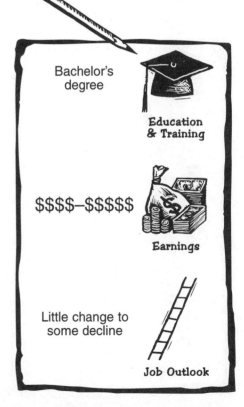

Bachelor's degree

Education & Training

$$$$–$$$$$

Earnings

Little change to some decline

Job Outlook

Inspectors & Compliance Officers, Except Construction

On the Job

Inspectors and compliance officers work to protect the public. Their duties vary widely. Some work with health and safety laws; others work with licensing, employment, and financial rules. Inspection officers check everything from food and water purity to airplane and car safety. Bank inspectors check out financial institutions, and customs inspectors enforce laws about what comes into and goes out of the country. Many travel frequently and some encounter dangerous situations.

Subjects to Study

Math, biology, chemistry, health, English, speech, writing skills

Discover More

Visit the meat section at your local grocery store. Ask the butcher about the store's inspection policy. Does the store buy only certain grades of meat? Does the butcher inspect the meat as well? How does the store assure that the meat it carries is healthy?

Related Jobs

Construction and building inspectors, fire marshals, police officers, FBI and Secret Service agents, and fish and game wardens

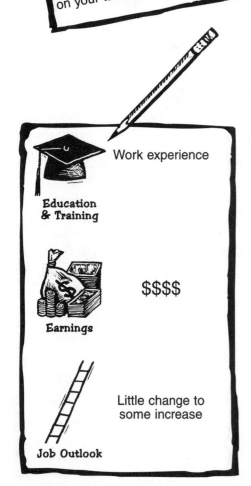

Work experience

Education & Training

$$$$

Earnings

Little change to some increase

Job Outlook

Insurance Underwriters

On the Job

How much should an insurance company charge for insurance? That depends on how likely a customer is to have an accident. Using national statistics, underwriters decide if a person applying for insurance is a good risk. They also help the company decide how much to charge. If they set the rates too low, the company will lose money. Too high, and the company will lose business to competitors.

Subjects to Study

Math, statistics, economics, English, business, speech, accounting

Discover More

Talk with an insurance agent in your community. Ask about the company's insurance rates. Are rates higher for those under 21? Are there other groups the company considers high-risk? Do people who live downtown pay higher rates than those in the suburbs? Are rates higher for people who own sports cars or minivans? Why?

Related Jobs

Auditors, budget analysts, financial advisors, loan officers, credit managers, real estate appraisers, and risk managers

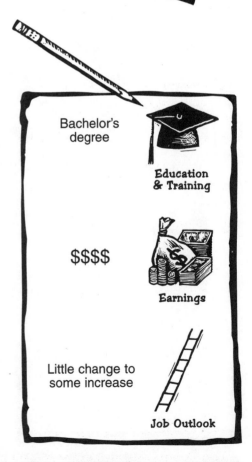

Bachelor's degree

Education & Training

$$$$

Earnings

Little change to some increase

Job Outlook

Loan Officers & Counselors

On the Job

When you apply for a loan, you must provide information on your work, your assets and debts, and your credit rating. A loan officer will meet with you and help you fill out the application. Then he or she looks through your information and helps the bank decide whether to loan you the money. Some loan counselors contact borrowers who are behind in repaying their loans and help them find a way of making payments.

Subjects to Study

Math, accounting, English, speech, writing and computer skills, business, and psychology

Discover More

Ask for a loan application from your parents' bank or credit union. Fill it out completely, including all of your sources of income, your savings, and your debts. Are you a good credit risk? Would you loan yourself money?

Related Jobs

Securities and financial services sales representatives, financial aid officers, real estate agents and brokers, and insurance agents and brokers

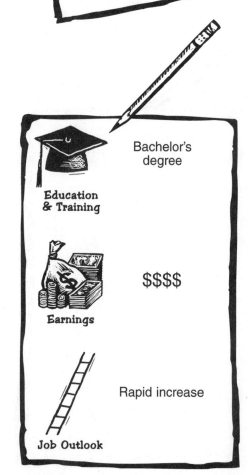

Education & Training
Bachelor's degree

Earnings
$$$$

Job Outlook
Rapid increase

Management Analysts & Consultants

On the Job

Management analysts and consultants are hired by companies to solve problems. The work varies with each client and from project to project. When a management team realizes there is a problem, it may call in a consultant to collect and review information, figure out where and why the problem is happening, and decide how to fix it. The job may require frequent traveling.

Something Extra

Do you have what it takes to be a consultant? Many consultants are self-employed. They work on contract for a business, helping management find the best way to solve a problem or make a product. When their work is done, they move on to the next client.

Consultants must be detail-oriented and enjoy working on their own.

Subjects to Study

English, math, business, economics, accounting, journalism, speech, writing and business skills

Discover More

Many consultants are self-employed. Interview people you know who are self-employed. How do they find their clients? Do they advertise? What do they like and dislike about being self-employed?

Related Jobs

Managers, computer systems analysts, operations research analysts, economists, and financial analysts

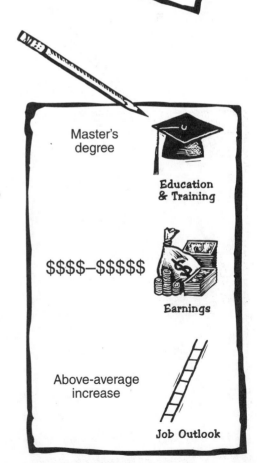

Master's degree

Education & Training

$$$$–$$$$$

Earnings

Above-average increase

Job Outlook

Marketing, Advertising, & Public Relations Managers

On the Job

These workers help businesses sell their products at a profit. Marketing managers decide whether a product will sell and who will buy it. Advertising managers decide what type of ads will work best. Promotion managers design campaigns to let the public know about the product. These managers travel a lot, and job transfers are common.

Subjects to Study

English, speech, writing skills, journalism, business, art

Discover More

The next time you are watching TV or reading a magazine, study the commercials or ads closely. Are they effective? Do they make you want to buy the products they are promoting? Design a poster advertising a school event.

Related Jobs

Art directors, commercial and graphic artists, copy chiefs, copywriters, editors, lobbyists, marketing research analysts, public relations specialists, sales representatives, and technical writers

Education & Training
Bachelor's degree +

Earnings
$$$$–$$$$$

Job Outlook
Rapid increase

Property Managers

On the Job

Property managers oversee apartment buildings, rental houses, businesses, and shopping malls. They sell empty space to renters, prepare leases, collect rent, and handle the bookkeeping. They also make sure the property is maintained, and they handle complaints from renters.

Something Extra

The next time you're at the mall, take a look around. Did you ever wonder who is in charge of all that open space? Property managers provide security, replace lightbulbs, hire cleaning crews, and make sure the lawns are mowed and the flowers are watered. They also collect rent from the stores and restaurants, and make sure the mall is clean, comfortable, and open for business.

Subjects to Study

Math, English, foreign languages, writing and computer skills, business, accounting, and shop courses

Discover More

Visit an apartment complex in your community and spend a day with the manager. Ask about the best and worst parts of the job, problems he or she sees in a typical week, and what kind of training you need for this job.

Related Jobs

Restaurant managers, hotel managers, health services managers, education administrators, and city managers

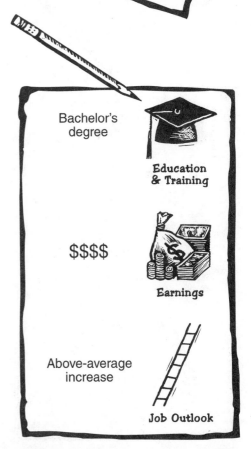

Bachelor's degree

Education & Training

$$$$

Earnings

Above-average increase

Job Outlook

Purchasers & Buyers

On the Job

Purchasers and buyers look for the best merchandise at the lowest price for their employers. They find the best products, negotiate the price, and make sure the right amount is received at the right time. They study sales records and inventory levels, identify suppliers, and stay aware of changes in the marketplace. Many spend several days a month traveling.

Subjects to Study

Math, business, economics, English, speech, home economics, computer skills

Discover More

Think of your family as a business. Help your parents compile a weekly "supplies" list. Then do some comparison shopping. Call or visit several stores to see who offers the best prices on the things your family needs. Will you save money if you buy in bulk? Should you buy from more than one source? How much can you save using coupons? See how much you can save your family business in one week.

Related Jobs

Retail sales workers, sales managers, marketing and advertising managers, manufacturers' and wholesale sales representatives, and insurance agents

Education & Training
Bachelor's degree +

Earnings
$$$$

Job Outlook
Little change to some increase

Restaurant & Food Service Managers

On the Job

Restaurant and food service managers select and price the food on a restaurant's menu. They hire and train workers and manage staffing, payroll, and bookkeeping. They also oversee the preparation of food, order supplies and ingredients, and make sure the restaurant is clean and well maintained. Many work nights and weekends, often under stressful circumstances.

Subjects to Study

Math, English, business, nutrition, home economics, psychology, accounting

Discover More

The best way to learn about the restaurant industry is to work in it. Consider taking a summer job at a local restaurant, waiting tables, busing tables, or washing dishes. Talk to someone who works in a restaurant.

Related Jobs

Hotel managers and assistants, health services administrators, retail store managers, and bank managers

Something Extra

Have you ever heard of Hamburger University? Students come from around the world to attend McDonald's manager training school in Oak Brook, Illinois.

There, they learn about maintaining product quality, hiring and supervising workers, advertising and publicity, equipment repair, and other aspects of restaurant management. The training lasts two weeks, and graduates are qualified to manage a McDonald's restaurant.

Work experience

Education & Training

$$$

Earnings

Rapid increase

Job Outlook

Professional & Technical Occupations

Aircraft Pilots

Something Extra

Sometimes a pilot's best attribute can be an ability to laugh at himself. After a particularly bumpy landing on one flight, the flight attendant addressed the passengers: "We ask that you please remain seated while Captain Kangaroo bounces us to the terminal!"

As the passengers left the plane, one elderly woman poked her head into the cabin and asked, "Sonny, did we land, or were we shot down?"

On the Job

Aircraft pilots fly airplanes and helicopters, test aircraft, and sometimes fight forest fires. Pilots may work for large airlines, charter services, the government, or private businesses. They must plan flights, check the aircraft and weather conditions, and keep records of each flight.

Education & Training

Long-term OJT to Voc/tech training +

Earnings

$$$$$

Job Outlook

Average increase

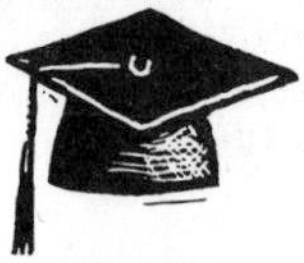

Subjects to Study

English, math, computer skills, electronics, geography, physics, physical education, foreign languages

Discover More

Take a tour with your class of your local airport. Visit the control tower, the maintenance hangar, and the cockpit of an airliner. Ask your tour guide about the skills pilots need. Are the requirements different for various airlines?

Related Jobs

Air traffic controllers and air traffic dispatchers

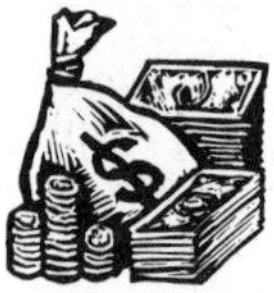

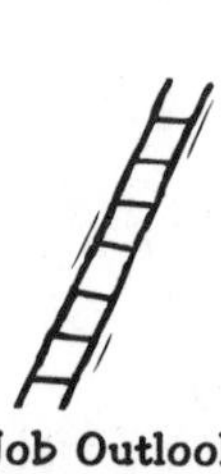

Air Traffic Controllers

On the Job

Air traffic controllers are responsible for the safe movement of airport traffic both in the air and on the ground. Using radar and visual observation, they direct landings, takeoffs, and ground movement of aircraft. They keep planes a safe distance apart during flights and tell pilots of current weather conditions. In emergencies they may search for missing aircraft. This can be a very stressful job.

Something Extra

Do you like computer games in which you have to keep track of a lot of small moving objects? Imagine each of those objects as a real-life aircraft, carrying real-live human beings. Your job is to keep track of them, ensure they remain safely apart, and stay aware of changing conditions that affect them. Air traffic controllers must be able to track several aircraft, monitor weather and traffic, and stay calm under sometimes extreme stress. People's lives depend on them!

Subjects to Study

English, math, computer skills, physics, shop and technology courses, foreign languages, electronics

Discover More

Call the U.S. Job Information Center in your area and ask for a copy of the Air Traffic Controller Announcement, which describes this job more fully. You can find the number in your Yellow Pages under U.S. Government, Office of Personnel Management.

Related Jobs

Airline-radio operators, aircraft pilots, and air traffic dispatchers

Long-term OJT

Education & Training

$$$$

Earnings

Little change

Job Outlook

Engineers

On the Job

Engineers design machinery, buildings, and highways, and develop new products and new ways of making products. Some engineers test the quality of products. Some supervise production in factories. They work in laboratories, factories, offices, and construction sites.

Subjects to Study

Math, physics, chemistry, shop and technology courses, drafting, computer skills

Discover More

Using Hot Wheels® racetrack pieces, try building a raceway down a steep slope. How steep can you make the slope before the cars fly off? Now put a curve at the bottom of the slope. What happens to the cars? How much must you tilt the curve to keep the cars on the track? These are the kinds of questions engineers answer.

Related Jobs

Physical scientists, life scientists, computer scientists, mathematicians, engineering and science technicians, and architects

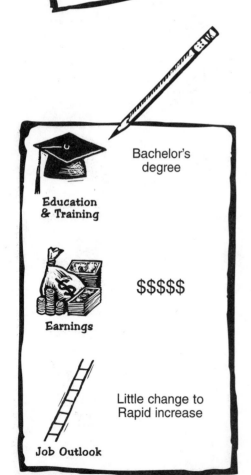

Education & Training
Bachelor's degree

Earnings
$$$$$

Job Outlook
Little change to Rapid increase

Aerospace Engineers

On the Job

Aerospace engineers design and test aircraft, missiles, and spacecraft. They develop new technology in aviation, defense systems, and space exploration. Some specialize in certain types of craft, such as helicopters, spacecraft, or rockets. States such as Texas, California, and Washington have the most jobs for aerospace engineers.

Something Extra

After an airline crash, aerospace engineers often are part of the team that is called in to find out what happened. They try to determine what caused the crash. To do this, they must "rebuild" the aircraft, piece by sometimes tiny piece. It is painstaking and time-consuming work, but it is crucial in preventing future crashes.

Subjects to Study

Math, physics, chemistry, computer technology, drafting, shop and technology courses

Discover More

You can learn more about aerospace engineering by building a model rocket with your teacher or another adult. What kind of fuel does the rocket use? Do different kits use different kinds of fuel? Which fuel works better?

Related Jobs

Scientists, mathematicians, engineering and science technicians, and other types of engineers

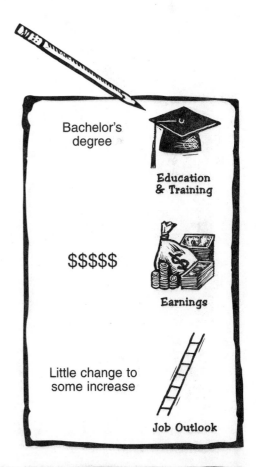

Bachelor's degree

Education & Training

$$$$$

Earnings

Little change to some increase

Job Outlook

Chemical Engineers

On the Job

Chemical engineers help make new chemicals and chemical products. They design equipment, plan how to make the products, and supervise production. They usually work in laboratories or factories. Some may be hired to help companies control pollution.

Subjects to Study

Math, physics, chemistry, biology, environmental science, computer science, shop and technology courses

Discover More

Get three pieces of white chalk. Put one into a glass container of lemon juice, one into a glass container of vinegar, and the third into a glass of tap water. Leave them alone for three days, then check on them. The acid lemon juice and vinegar will break down the chalk, in the same way that acid rain causes erosion.

Related Jobs

Scientists, mathematicians, engineering and science technicians, architects, and other engineers

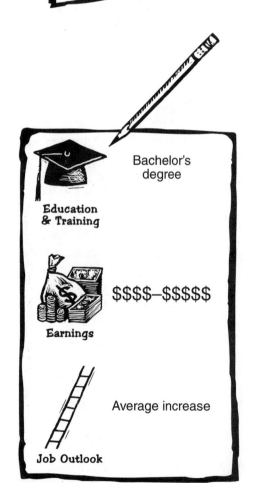

Education & Training — Bachelor's degree

Earnings — $$$$–$$$$$

Job Outlook — Average increase

Civil Engineers

On the Job

Civil engineers design and supervise the building of roads, bridges, tunnels, airports, sewer systems, and buildings. Some civil engineers work in research or teach other engineers. Most work in large industrial cities, but some projects may be in isolated places or foreign countries. Civil engineers often move from place to place working on different projects.

Something Extra

In California and Japan, where earthquakes are a constant threat, engineers must design buildings with earthquakes in mind. In places near the ocean, such as Florida and Texas, they have a different hazard to plan for—hurricanes. What special hazards would an engineer in your area have to keep in mind?

Subjects to Study

Math, physics, drafting, computer science, shop and technology courses, environmental science, geology, foreign languages

Discover More

Using craft sticks, glue, paper clips, and rubber bands, build a bridge at least a foot long. Can you make it strong enough to support a one-pound weight? How many supports must you use? Does the glue hold, or do you need extra holding support? Now try a two-foot span.

Related Jobs

Scientists, mathematicians, engineering and science technicians, architects, and other engineers

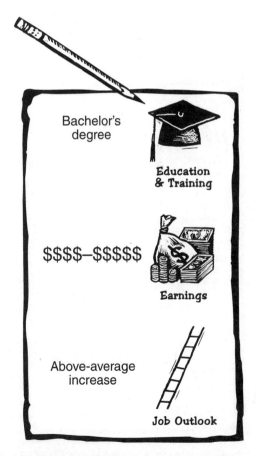

Bachelor's degree

Education & Training

$$$$–$$$$$

Earnings

Above-average increase

Job Outlook

Electrical & Electronics Engineers

On the Job

Electrical and electronics engineers design, test, and supervise the making of electrical equipment like generators and motors, wiring in cars, computers, and video equipment. They also solve problems involved with using this equipment. They determine how long a project will take to complete and how much it will cost.

Subjects to Study

Math, chemistry, physics, computer science, drafting, shop and technology courses

Discover More

Static electricity is all around us. Try this experiment on a cool, dry day. Fill a balloon with air. Rub it against your hair for about 15 seconds. What happens to your hair? Try moving the balloon nearer and then away from your head. Can you make your hair stand on end? That's static electricity.

Related Jobs

Scientists, mathematicians, engineering and science technicians, architects, and other engineers

Education & Training
Bachelor's degree

Earnings
$$$$–$$$$$

Job Outlook
Rapid increase

Industrial Engineers

On the Job

Industrial engineers find the best ways to use people, machines, and materials to make a product. They help companies make the best products for the least amount of money. They may help a business owner decide where to build a new factory or how to set up an assembly line. They are the bridge between management and operations. Computers help them do faster work and save money.

Something Extra

What kinds of companies employ industrial engineers? Almost every kind that manufactures a product—from toy makers to car makers, garment makers to gun makers. Any company that produces an object for sale might employ an industrial engineer to help decide the best way to set up an assembly line, the best way to put a product together, or the best place to set up a new factory.

Subjects to Study

Math, computer science, physics, shop and technology courses, drafting

Discover More

Set up an assembly-line operation to build a simple craft—for example, a gingerbread house. Where would you place the gingerbread pieces? How about the icing and decorations? Which workers will do which jobs? How quickly can they move a house through the line from start to finish?

Related Jobs

Scientists, mathematicians, engineering and science technicians, architects, and other engineers

Bachelor's degree

Education & Training

$$$$–$$$$$

Earnings

Average increase

Job Outlook

Mechanical Engineers

On the Job

Mechanical engineers design engines, machines, and other mechanical equipment. Some design rocket engines, robots, and refrigerators. They also design tools that other engineers use in their work. Most work for companies in the manufacturing industry. They use computers to help in their work.

Subjects to Study

Math, physics, drafting, computer science, shop and technology courses

Discover More

Hold a class "invention convention." Give everyone in your class the same set of objects. You might have some paper clips, wood pieces, rubber bands, strips of paper, glue, or other items. Now see what each of you can make from the items in half an hour. Whose invention is the most creative? The most useful? The most useless?

Related Jobs

Scientists, mathematicians, engineering and science technicians, architects, and other engineers

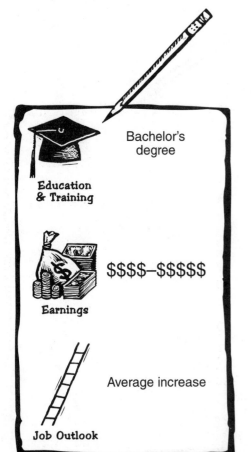

Education & Training
Bachelor's degree

Earnings
$$$$–$$$$$

Job Outlook
Average increase

Metallurgical, Ceramic, & Materials Engineers

On the Job

These engineers develop new kinds of metals, ceramics, and other materials to do special jobs. They also study and test metals to make new products, such as the materials now being used in "stealth bombers." They might also look for ways to make a metal stronger without making it heavier. Most of these engineers work in private industry and must wear protective clothing and goggles on the job.

Something Extra

You may have ceramic tile in the shower at your house. But did you know it's also been used in outer space? The space shuttle is covered with special ceramic tiles that keep it from overheating. Without the protection of these tiles, the shuttle would burn up when it reentered the earth's atmosphere.

Subjects to Study

Math, chemistry, physics, drafting, English, shop and technology courses

Discover More

Visit a pottery shop in your area, or arrange for a potter to visit your class. Try making a pot or vase using a pottery wheel. Does adjusting the speed of the wheel affect your work? Is it easier to make a small, rounded pot or a taller, slender one?

Related Jobs

Scientists, mathematicians, engineering and science technicians, architects, and other engineers

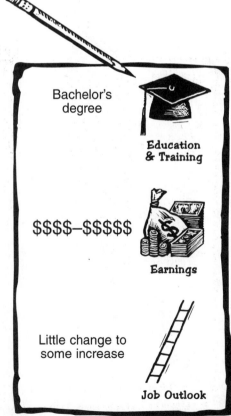

Bachelor's degree

Education & Training

$$$$–$$$$$

Earnings

Little change to some increase

Job Outlook

Mining Engineers

On the Job

Mining engineers find, remove, and prepare metals and minerals for industries. They make sure that mines, tunnels, and open pits are safe for workers and that mining operations don't damage the environment. Many specialize in mining one mineral, such as gold or coal. Some design new mining equipment. They may work in very dangerous conditions.

Subjects to Study

Math, physics, geology, chemistry, environmental science, drafting, shop and technology courses, computer skills

Discover More

Geology is the study of the earth. Try making a collection of rocks from your area. Can you identify them? What do they tell you about the ground under your feet?

Related Jobs

Scientists, mathematicians, engineering and science technicians, architects, and other engineers

Education & Training
Bachelor's degree

Earnings
$$$$–$$$$$

Job Outlook
Declining

Nuclear Engineers

On the Job

Nuclear engineers study nuclear energy and radiation. They design and operate nuclear power plants that provide electricity and power Navy ships. Other nuclear engineers develop nuclear weapons or study uses of radiation in industry and medicine. Many work for the federal government.

Something Extra

A meltdown is the worst accident that can happen at a nuclear reactor. In a meltdown, the radioactive material becomes so hot it melts some or all of the fuel in the reactor. If radiation gets into the environment, it is dangerous to all living things. After the Chernobyl nuclear accident in the former USSR, cancer rates in the affected area rose dramatically.

Subjects to Study

Math, chemistry, physics, drafting, biology, environmental studies, computer science, shop and technology courses

Discover More

Nuclear workers deal with properties of physics. Try this physics experiment. Take an empty soup can with the lid removed. Poke a hole in the side of the can near the bottom. Watching out for sharp edges, hold your finger over the hole and fill the can with water. Now turn out the lights and put a flashlight over the top of the can. Take your finger off the hole and watch the water pour out. Did you bend the light?

Related Jobs

Scientists, mathematicians, engineering and science technicians, architects, and other engineers

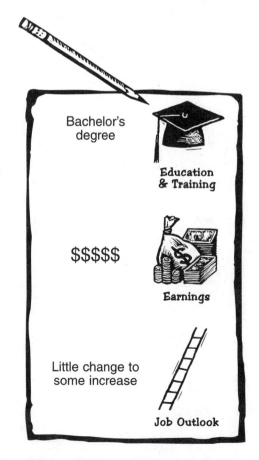

Bachelor's degree

Education & Training

$$$$$

Earnings

Little change to some increase

Job Outlook

Petroleum Engineers

On the Job

Petroleum engineers look for oil and natural gas and find the best ways to get it from the earth. Many work in states that have large deposits of fossil fuels, such as Texas, Oklahoma, Louisiana, and California. Some work at offshore oil-drilling sites. Others work in oil-producing countries such as Saudi Arabia.

Subjects to Study

Math, geology, chemistry, physics, environmental studies, biology, computer science, shop and technology courses

Discover More

Do you know why an oil spill is so bad for the environment? It's because oil floats on top of water instead of mixing in and dissolving. Try this experiment and see for yourself. Put food color in a bowl of water, then pour vegetable oil on top. Does the oil mix?

Related Jobs

Scientists, mathematicians, engineering and science technicians, architects, and other engineers

Education & Training — Bachelor's degree

Earnings — $$$$$

Job Outlook — Little change

Engineering Technicians

On the Job

Engineering technicians use science, engineering, and math to solve problems for businesses. They help engineers and scientists with experiments and develop models of new equipment. Some supervise production workers or check the quality of products. Like engineers, they specialize in an area such as mechanics, electronics, or chemicals. Some may be exposed to hazards from equipment, chemicals, or toxic materials.

Subjects to Study

Math, physics, chemistry, electronics, shop and technology courses, drafting

Discover More

What's the simplest way to boil an egg? Easy, right? Just put the egg in a pan of boiling water and cook it. Now think about the reverse. How complicated can you make the job? On paper, draw an egg-boiling machine. Make it as complicated and ridiculous as you can.

Related Jobs

Science technicians, drafters, surveyors, broadcast technicians, and health technologists and technicians

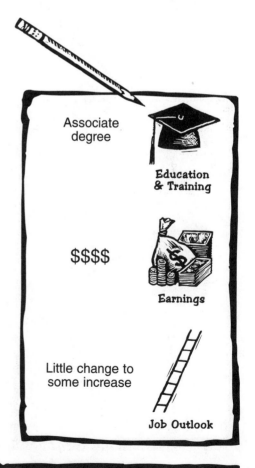

Associate degree

Education & Training

$$$$

Earnings

Little change to some increase

Job Outlook

Architects

On the Job

Architects design buildings and other structures. They make sure buildings are functional, safe, and economical. They draw plans of every part of a building, including the plumbing and electrical systems. They also help choose a building site and decide what materials to use. Most architects today use computers in their work.

Subjects to Study

Math, English, writing skills, communication skills, drawing courses, drafting, computer courses, shop and technology courses

Discover More

What does your dream house look like? Using graph paper, draw a room-by-room floor plan of your ideal home. Include all the elements you'd like—maybe a fireplace, an exercise room, a game room, or a spa. Don't forget the practical rooms—everyone needs a kitchen and a bath!

Related Jobs

Landscape architects, building contractors, civil engineers, urban planners, interior designers, industrial designers, drafters, and graphic designers

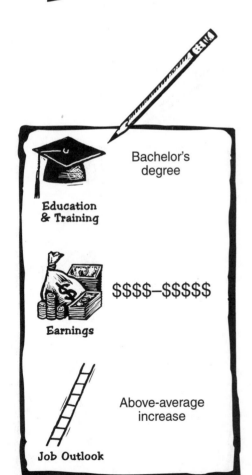

Bachelor's degree

Education & Training

$$$$–$$$$$

Earnings

Above-average increase

Job Outlook

Drafters

On the Job

Drafters prepare the drawings used to build everything from spacecraft to bridges. Using rough sketches done by others, they produce detailed technical drawings with specific information to create a finished product. Drafters use handbooks, tables, calculators, and computers to do their work. Many specialize in architecture, electronics, or aeronautics.

Something Extra

Drafters today use computer-aided drafting (CAD) systems to create drawings on a video screen. When CAD systems were first introduced, many people thought a new occupation (CAD operator) would result. But now it is obvious that people still need drafting skills to use the CAD system. Drafters today need both drawing and computer skills to do their jobs.

Subjects to Study

Math, physics, drafting, art courses, computer skills, English, shop and technology courses

Discover More

Try making your own drawing of a building or some kind of machine. You can use either paper and pencil or a computer drawing program. You can find books about drafting at the library.

Related Jobs

Architects, landscape architects, engineers, engineering technicians, science technicians, cartographers, and surveyors

Voc/tech training

Education & Training

$$$–$$$$

Earnings

Little change to some increase

Job Outlook

Landscape Architects

On the Job

Landscape architects make areas such as parks, malls, and golf courses beautiful and useful. They decide where the buildings, roads, and walkways will go, and how the flower gardens and trees should be arranged. They create designs, estimate costs, and check that the plans are being carried out correctly. Some are self-employed.

Subjects to Study

Math, botany, ecology, drafting, art, geology, communications, computer skills

Discover More

Design a flower garden that will grow in your area's climate. What colors do you want? Should you use tall plants, short ones, or a combination? Do you want all spring-bloomers or plants that will bloom at various times? Check catalogs and local nurseries for prices. How much will your garden cost? How much maintenance will it need?

Related Jobs

Architects, interior designers, civil engineers, urban and regional planners, botanists, and horticulturists

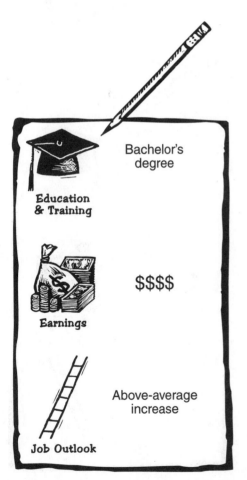

Education & Training
Bachelor's degree

Earnings
$$$$

Job Outlook
Above-average increase

Surveyors & Mapping Scientists

On the Job

Surveyors measure and map the earth's surface to set official land, air, and water boundaries. They may check old legal documents for information and write reports. They work outdoors in all kinds of weather and may travel long distances to work sites. Mapping scientists use the information surveyors gather to prepare maps and charts.

Something Extra

Satellites are changing the way surveyors work today. A "Global Positioning System" uses radio signals from satellites to locate points on the earth. The surveyor places a radio receiver about the size of a backpack at the desired point, and can collect information from several satellites at once. The receiver can be placed in a car to trace a road system.

Subjects to Study

Algebra, geometry, trigonometry, drafting, mechanical drawing, computer science, English, writing skills, geography, geology

Discover More

Make a map of your neighborhood, showing how to get from your house to your school. Include all streets and important landmarks, bodies of water or forests, malls or business districts, parks and playgrounds—anything that acts as a landmark in your area. If you gave someone at school your map, could the person get to your house?

Related Jobs

Civil engineers, architects, geologists, geophysicists, geographers, and urban planners

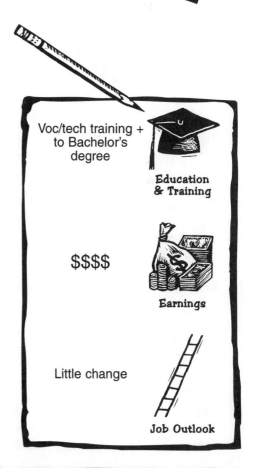

Voc/tech training +
to Bachelor's degree

Education & Training

$$$$

Earnings

Little change

Job Outlook

Actuaries

On the Job

Actuaries design insurance plans that will help their company make a profit. They study statistics and social trends to decide how much money an insurance company should charge for an insurance policy. They predict the amount of money an insurance company will have to pay to its customers for claims. Some actuaries are self-employed and work as consultants.

Subjects to Study

Math, calculus, accounting, computer science, writing skills

Discover More

Take a survey in your class. How many of your classmates have broken a bone or sprained an ankle? How many have stayed overnight in a hospital? How many have had their tonsils or appendix removed? Now separate the answers by boys and girls. Which group has had more medical emergencies?

Related Jobs

Accountants, economists, financial analysts, mathematicians, risk managers, and statisticians

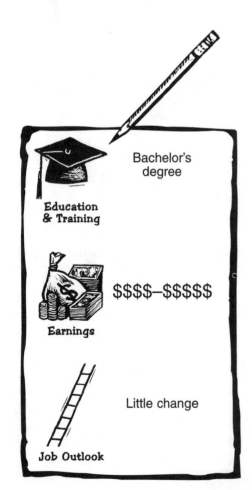

Education & Training
Bachelor's degree

Earnings
$$$$–$$$$$

Job Outlook
Little change

Computer Programmers

On the Job

Computer programmers write, update, test, and maintain the software that makes computers work. They provide detailed, step-by-step instructions for the computer. If the software does not produce the desired result, the programmer must correct the errors until the program works effectively. Some may work nights so that the computers they work on are available to businesses during the day.

Subjects to Study

Computer skills, computer programming, data processing, math, physics, keyboarding, electronics

Discover More

The image you see on a computer monitor is made up of thousands of tiny dots. Color monitors use red, green, and blue dots. Use a magnifying glass to look at the screen, or use a drop of water to act like a lens. Get a tiny drop of water on your fingertip and touch it to your computer screen. (Be careful not to drip!) Do you see the dots?

Related Jobs

Statisticians, engineers, financial analysts, accountants, auditors, actuaries, and operations research analysts

Voc/tech training to Bachelor's degree

Education & Training

$$$$

Earnings

Above-average increase

Job Outlook

Computer Scientists, Computer Engineers, & Systems Analysts

On the Job

Computer scientists and engineers do research, design computers, and find new ways to use them in business. Systems analysts identify problems in business, science, and engineering. Then they use computers to solve the problems. This kind of work can result in eye strain, backaches, and hand and wrist problems.

Subjects to Study

Math, physics, computer science, communication skills, shop and technology courses

Discover More

Did you know your computer gives out radio waves? Try this experiment and see. Get a small radio and set it on AM. Turn it on and find a spot between stations, so you just receive static. Now turn the radio up high and put it next to your computer. You should hear sounds from your computer on the radio!

Related Jobs

Computer programmers, financial analysts, urban planners, engineers, operations research analysts, management analysts, and actuaries

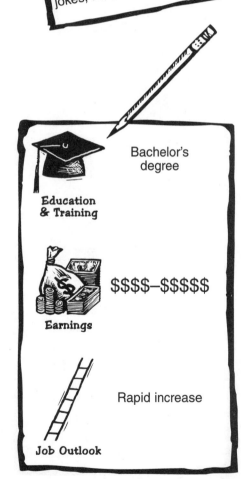

Education & Training
Bachelor's degree

Earnings
$$$$–$$$$$

Job Outlook
Rapid increase

Mathematicians

On the Job

Mathematicians work in two areas: theory and applications. *Theoretical mathematicians* look for relationships between new math principles and old ones. This can help in science and engineering. *Applied mathematicians* use math to solve problems in business, government, and everyday life. Many mathematicians teach at colleges and universities.

Something Extra

Do you know what a graph is? It's a mathematical model made of dots and connecting lines. Graph theory, a kind of mathematics, is the study of graphs. And it's used for more than you might imagine. Mathematicians use graph theory to design computer networks, to help in urban planning, to route and schedule airline traffic, and to write unbreakable codes for the military.

Subjects to Study

Math, algebra, geometry, trigonometry, calculus, logic, computer science, physics, statistics

Discover More

To try your hand at some fun and challenging math activities, visit the Internet School Library Media Center at http://falcon.jmu.edu/~ramseyil/index.html

Related Jobs

Actuaries, statisticians, and computer programmers

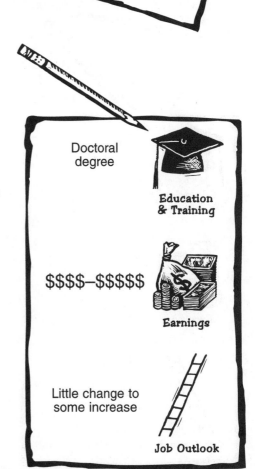

Doctoral degree

Education & Training

$$$$–$$$$$

Earnings

Little change to some increase

Job Outlook

Operations Research Analysts

On the Job

Operations research analysts help businesses operate efficiently by applying mathematical principles to problems. First, analysts define and study the problem. Next, they gather information by talking with people and choosing which model they will use. Finally, they present their findings and recommendations to the company's management.

Subjects to Study

Math, statistics, computer skills, English, communication skills, logic

Discover More

Take a walk through your school building. Now, using graph paper, make a map of the building, including all the classrooms, offices, restrooms, cafeteria, and exits. Using your map, plot out the most direct, effective way to deliver "mail" to each classroom and office. Then plot out the most efficient exit route from each classroom.

Related Jobs

Computer scientists, applied mathematicians, statisticians, economists, and managerial occupations

Education & Training — Master's degree

Earnings — $$$$–$$$$$

Job Outlook — Little change to some increase

Statisticians

On the Job

Statisticians collect information from surveys and experiments. They decide where and how to gather the information, who to survey, and what questions to ask. They use the information they collect to make predictions about the economy or to assess various social problems. This helps business and government leaders make decisions.

Subjects to Study

Math, algebra, statistics, economics, business, sciences, computer skills, communication skills

Discover More

Telemarketing—calling people on the phone—is one way to conduct a survey. Check the want ads of your local newspaper for telemarketing job openings. Can you tell which companies need people to sell products and which ones need workers to gather information?

Related Jobs

Actuaries, mathematicians, operations research analysts, computer programmers, computer systems analysts, engineers, economists, financial analysts, life scientists, physical scientists, and social scientists

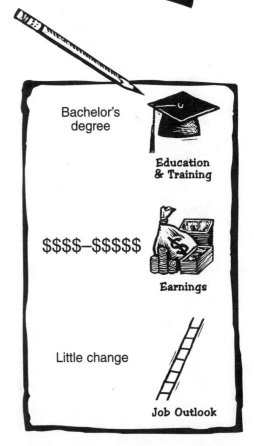

Bachelor's degree

Education & Training

$$$$–$$$$$

Earnings

Little change

Job Outlook

Agricultural Scientists

On the Job

Agricultural scientists study farm crops and animals. They look for ways to control pests and weeds safely, increase crop yields with less labor, and save water and soil. They also look for ways to make healthy, attractive food products for consumers. Agricultural scientists specialize in food, plant, soil, or animal science. Many work outdoors in all kinds of weather.

Subjects to Study

Biology, environmental science, physics, chemistry, communication skills, math, business, life sciences, nutrition, home economics

Discover More

Set up a growing experiment of your own. Choose a plant and get a package of seeds at a garden center. Now plant the seeds in four containers. Put two containers on a sunny window sill and two in a shady spot. Water one in the window and one in the shade every day. Water the other two only once every four or five days. Which seeds grow best?

Related Jobs

Chemists, physicists, farmers and farm managers, foresters, conservation scientists, veterinarians, landscape architects, and soil scientists

Education & Training
Bachelor's degree

Earnings
$$$$

Job Outlook
Above-average increase

Biological & Medical Scientists

On the Job

Biological and medical scientists study living things and their environment. They do research, develop new medicines, increase crop amounts, and improve the environment. Some study specialty areas such as ocean life, plant life, or animal life. They may work in clinics or hospitals, or travel to primitive places to do research.

Something Extra

Did you know that people once thought smoking was good for you? Early TV ads promoted smoking cigarettes as a refreshing, healthy way to relax. It took medical scientists to prove that smoking puts people at risk for lung cancer and heart disease.
Supplying information is one way medical scientists help people live longer, healthier lives.

Subjects to Study

Math, English, biology, botany, chemistry, physics, communication skills, computer skills, nutrition

Discover More

Study the effects of acid rain on plant life. Get two small potted plants from a garden center. Keep them in the same place. Water one daily with regular tap water. Water the other daily with "acid rain" you make by adding ½ teaspoon white vinegar to 2½ teaspoons of tap water. Which plant grows better?

Related Jobs

Foresters, range managers, animal breeders, horticulturists, soil scientists, life science technicians, medical doctors, dentists, and veterinarians

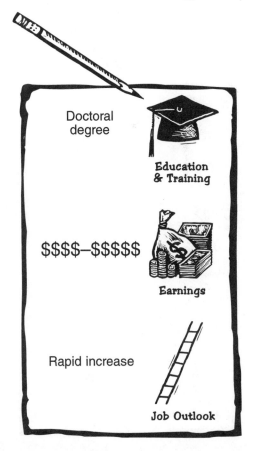

Doctoral degree

Education & Training

$$$$–$$$$$

Earnings

Rapid increase

Job Outlook

Foresters & Conservation Scientists

On the Job

Foresters and conservation scientists manage, use, and protect natural resources such as water, wood, and wildlife. Foresters supervise the use of timber for lumber companies. Range managers oversee and protect rangelands so the environment is not damaged. Soil conservationists help farmers save the soil, water, and other natural resources. All of these workers spend time outdoors in all kinds of weather.

Subjects to Study

Math, chemistry, biology, botany, ecology, agriculture, computer science, economics, business

Discover More

Acid rain is a serious problem in some parts of the U.S. You can test for acid rain in your area using the testing paper described under "Chemists." The next time it rains, collect rainwater in a clean cup. Put a strip of testing paper in the water and watch it change colors. Is the rain in your area acidic? (For directions on how to make testing paper, see page 655.)

Related Jobs

Agricultural scientists, biological scientists, environmental scientists, farmers and farm managers, ranchers, soil scientists, and wildlife managers

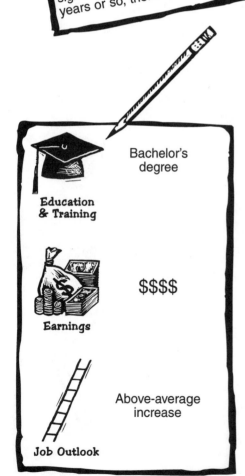

Education & Training
Bachelor's degree

Earnings
$$$$

Job Outlook
Above-average increase

Chemists

On the Job

Chemists look for and use new information about chemicals. They develop new paints, fibers, adhesives, drugs, and other products. They develop processes that save energy and reduce pollution. They make improvements in agriculture, medicine, and food processing. Most work in manufacturing firms or teach at colleges and universities. Their work can sometimes be dangerous.

Something Extra

What would the world be like without chemists? It's hard to imagine. For starters, there would be no plastic, no nylon, no acrylic paint, no glue, no fiberglass. Our houses wouldn't have aluminum siding, our pantyhose would be expensive silk, our hospitals would be empty of medicines, and our cars (if they existed at all) would have wooden wheels! Chemists make the materials that make the modern world work.

Subjects to Study

Math, physics, chemistry, biology, computer science, English, business

Discover More

Make your own acid-testing paper. Boil red cabbage leaves for 15 minutes. Drain the leaves, saving the water. Cut a paper towel into strips and soak the strips in the cabbage water. Spread the strips out on newspaper to dry, then use them to test for acidity. Dip the strips into liquids. If they turn pink, the liquid is an acid. If they turn green, it is a base.

Related Jobs

Chemical engineers, agricultural scientists, biological scientists, chemical technicians, and physical and life scientists

Bachelor's degree

Education & Training

$$$$

Earnings

Above-average increase

Job Outlook

Geologists & Geophysicists

On the Job

Geologists and geophysicists study the earth. They look at rocks, collect information, and make maps. Many search for oil, natural gas, minerals, and underground water. They play an important role in cleaning up the earth's environment, designing waste disposal sites, and cleaning up polluted land and water. They may work outdoors and travel to remote areas or overseas.

Subjects to Study

Math, computer science, chemistry, physics, geology

Discover More

Earthquakes happen when tectonic plates of the earth's surface move. You can see the same effect by cracking the shell of a hard-boiled egg. The thin shell represents the earth's crust, moving around on the slippery mantle. Move the pieces of shell around. What happens when they collide? Earthquake!

Related Jobs

Engineering technicians, science technicians, petroleum engineers, surveyors and mapping scientists, life scientists, physicists, chemists, meteorologists, mathematicians, computer scientists, and soil scientists

Education & Training
Bachelor's degree

Earnings
$$$$–$$$$$

Job Outlook
Average increase

Meteorologists

On the Job

Meteorologists study the atmosphere—the air that covers the earth—for its effects on our environment. The most well-known area of their work is weather forecasting. They also study trends in the earth's climate and apply their research to air-pollution control, air and sea transportation, and defense. Meteorologists often work nights, weekends, and holidays at weather stations.

Subjects to Study

Math, chemistry, physics, computer science, statistics, environmental science

Discover More

Contact a local TV station in your area and ask to become one of its "weather watchers." Hang a thermometer outside—a little way away from your home. Take daily readings. Place a large, rimmed dish on a flat surface outside to measure rain or snowfall. Call your reports in to the TV station, and watch the weather report for your information.

Related Jobs

Geologists and geophysicists, civil and environmental engineers, and oceanographers

Something Extra

In 1969, when Hurricane Camille slammed into the rural Mississippi coast with winds topping 200 miles per hour, it killed 140 people. The resulting floods and mudslides killed another 113. In 1992, when Hurricane Andrew ripped through southern Florida, newscasters feared the death toll would be even higher. Surprisingly, only 15 people were killed by Andrew. Why? Meteorologists had given people advance warning and time to prepare, saving hundreds of lives.

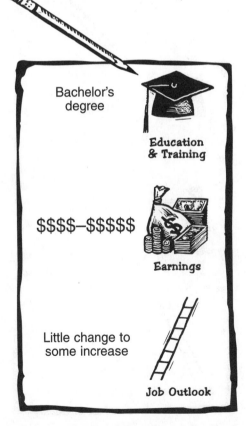

Bachelor's degree

Education & Training

$$$$–$$$$$

Earnings

Little change to some increase

Job Outlook

Physicists & Astronomers

On the Job

Physicists study the matter that makes up the universe. They also study forces of nature like gravity and nuclear interaction. They use their studies to design medical equipment, electronic devices, and lasers. Astronomers study the moon, sun, planets, galaxies, and stars. Their knowledge is used in space flight and navigation. Many teach in colleges and universities.

Subjects to Study

Math, physics, chemistry, computer science, geology, astronomy

Discover More

Try this simple experiment: Set a one-foot plate of plexiglass up on wooden blocks on a table, so that the plate is 1 to 3 inches above the table. Now put a handful of Rice Krispies® cereal on the table. Rub the top of the plexiglass quickly with a piece of wool. The cereal will stand on end, then "jump" from table to plexiglass and back again.

Related Jobs

Chemists, geologists and geophysicists, engineers, engineering and science technicians, and mathematicians

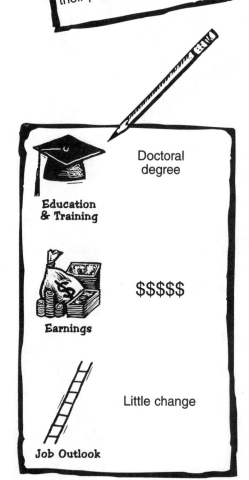

Education & Training
Doctoral degree

Earnings
$$$$$

Job Outlook
Little change

Science Technicians

On the Job

Science technicians use science and math to solve research problems. They also investigate, invent, and help improve products. They set up, operate, and maintain lab equipment, monitor experiments, and record results. They may specialize in agriculture, biology, chemistry, or other sciences. Some work outdoors and may be exposed to chemicals or radiation.

Something Extra

Finding new uses for agricultural crops can be important to areas that grow those crops. George Washington Carver's work is an excellent example of this. Carver, the son of slaves, developed hundreds of uses for two Southern crops: the peanut and the sweet potato. His work helped the South's economy and made him a nationally recognized scientist.

Subjects to Study

Math, physics, chemistry, biology, geology, shop and technology courses, computer science

Discover More

Science technicians need good eye-hand coordination and a good ability to follow written instructions. You can hone your skills by putting together model cars or model ships. Are the directions in the kit clear and easy to follow? How would you change them to make them clearer?

Related Jobs

Engineering technicians, broadcast technicians, drafters, health technologists and technicians, and agriculture and forestry workers

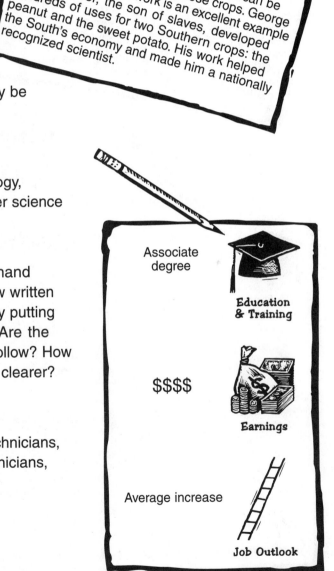

Associate degree

Education & Training

$$$$

Earnings

Average increase

Job Outlook

Lawyers & Judges

On the Job

Lawyers give people advice about the law and their rights. They represent people in court, presenting evidence that supports a client's position, asking questions, and arguing their case. Judges oversee trials and make sure that everyone follows the court rules. In court cases without a jury, the judge decides the verdict.

Subjects to Study

English, writing skills, public speaking, government, history, foreign languages, psychology, computer science, logic

Discover More

Organize a class debate. Pick a topic you feel strongly about, take a position, and argue your side. Be sure you do some research first—read articles and books on the topic and find out what other people think of it. Can you change your opponent's mind?

Related Jobs

Paralegals, journalists, title examiners, legislators, lobbyists, FBI special agents, political officeholders, and corporate executives

Education & Training
Professional degree

Earnings
$$$$–$$$$$

Job Outlook
Average increase

Paralegals

On the Job

Paralegals help lawyers prepare their cases. They do research and write reports that lawyers use to present their arguments in court. They may meet with clients to get information about a case, but they do not argue cases in court or set fees. Some paralegals have a wide variety of tasks, while others specialize in one area.

Something Extra

Paralegals today use computers to do their research. Special software packages and the Internet put a world of information at their fingertips. They simply enter a topic and receive a list of all documents on that subject. They also use computers to organize the volumes of paper needed to support cases. These programs help today's paralegals do in one day work that used to take weeks!

Subjects to Study

English, business courses, keyboarding, computer and writing skills, foreign languages, logic

Discover More

Contact a law firm or a legal aid society in your area. Ask to talk to a paralegal. Find out what his or her duties involve. Ask how he or she became interested in the occupation and what kind of training the job requires.

Related Jobs

Abstractors, claim examiners, compliance and enforcement inspectors, occupational safety and health workers, patent agents, police officers, and title examiners

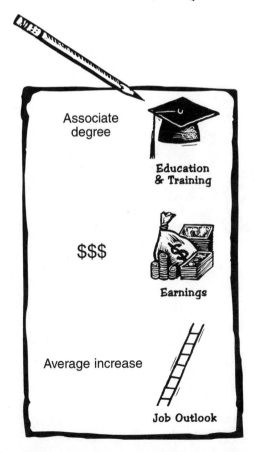

Associate degree

Education & Training

$$$

Earnings

Average increase

Job Outlook

Economists & Marketing Research Analysts

On the Job

Economists study how people use resources like land, labor, raw materials, and machinery to make products. They use their studies to advise businesses and government agencies. Marketing research analysts tell businesses about the best ways to sell a product based on information they gather through interviews and questionnaires. Some analysts are self-employed and travel to work for different clients.

Subjects to Study

Math, English, economics, business, statistics, computer science, psychology, accounting

Discover More

Take a survey in your class. Buy several different kinds of tortilla chips, then do a blind taste test. Blindfold several classmates, then have them taste the chips. Keep a tally of which ones they prefer. Ask why they prefer one brand over another. These are the kinds of market surveys analysts perform.

Related Jobs

Financial managers, financial analysts, accountants and auditors, underwriters, actuaries, securities and financial services sales workers, credit analysts, loan officers, and budget officers

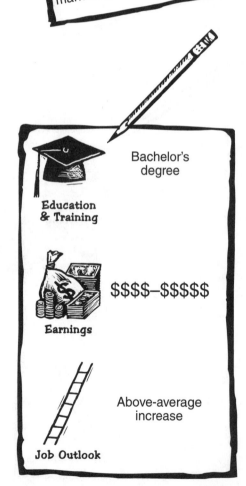

Education & Training — Bachelor's degree

Earnings — $$$$–$$$$$

Job Outlook — Above-average increase

Psychologists

On the Job

Psychologists study the way people think, feel, and act. They work to understand, explain, and change people's behavior. They may conduct training programs, do market research, or provide counseling. They may also work with mentally ill individuals. Psychologists work with schools, businesses, and health-care centers to help people deal with stress and changes in their lives, such as divorce and aging.

Something Extra

Psychologists sometimes use hypnosis to help people. They put a client into a deep trance and then make suggestions for changing a problem behavior. While the person may not remember the suggestions when he or she is awake, they are planted deep in the subconscious and are triggered by the problem behavior. Hypnosis can be useful for people who want to quit smoking, lose weight, or overcome a fear.

Subjects to Study

English, psychology, statistics, communication skills, biology, physical sciences, computer science, writing skills

Discover More

Try this experiment: Get a small fish in a bowl. Feed it at the same time every day. Each time you feed the fish, just before you put the food in the water, tap on the side of the bowl. Soon, when your fish sees you tap on the bowl, it will look for food on the water's surface. That's called *conditioning*.

Related Jobs

Psychiatrists, social workers, sociologists, clergy, special education teachers, and counselors

Master's degree to Doctoral degree

Education & Training

$$$$–$$$$$

Earnings

Little change to some increase

Job Outlook

Urban & Regional Planners

On the Job

Urban and regional planners develop programs that encourage growth in certain communities and regions. They make plans for the best use of land and study the area's schools, hospitals, parks, roads, and other facilities to see if they meet the needs of the community. They also deal with legal codes and environmental issues.

Subjects to Study

Math, English, public speaking, government, psychology, writing skills, computer science, sociology

Discover More

Plan out a town on graph paper. Include all the roads, houses, schools, churches, and parks. Don't forget hospitals, police and fire stations, gas stations, a shopping district, and a town center.

Related Jobs

Architects, landscape architects, city managers, civil engineers, environmental engineers, and geographers

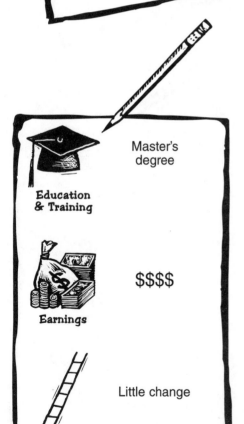

Education & Training
Master's degree

Earnings
$$$$

Job Outlook
Little change

Recreation Workers

On the Job

Recreation workers often work as camp counselors or coaches, organizing leisure activities at parks, health clubs, camps, tourist sites, and other places. They teach people how to use recreation equipment properly and safely. They often work nights and weekends. Recreation workers may work in state and national parks, health clubs, or even cruise ships. Many work part-time.

Something Extra

People from all walks of life can get a taste of the wilderness with Outward Bound Schools. Teenagers, senior citizens, school groups, and business groups can take two-week treks into the mountains. There, they go hiking, white-water rafting, rock climbing, and backcountry skiing. Outward Bound trainers help the adventurers build their self-confidence and their teamwork, while making sure they are safe.

Subjects to Study

English, communication skills, business, accounting, physical education, swimming, art, music, drama, sports

Discover More

Call your local YMCA, YWCA, Boys' or Girls' Club, or community center and volunteer to help out. You might be asked to watch younger children, teach them games, or help maintain equipment.

Related Jobs

Recreational therapists, social workers, parole officers, human relations counselors, school counselors, psychologists, and teachers

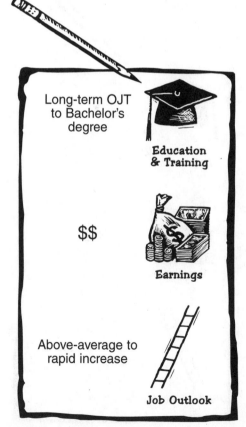

Long-term OJT to Bachelor's degree

Education & Training

$$

Earnings

Above-average to rapid increase

Job Outlook

Social & Human Service Assistants

On the Job

Social and human service assistants are in the business of helping people. They might work in a food bank, train mentally handicapped adults to do a job, supervise teenagers in a group home, or help Alzheimer's patients in a day program. They evaluate clients' needs, help them fill out the paperwork to get benefits, keep records, and file reports with social service agencies. They work in offices, hospitals, group homes, and private agencies.

Subjects to Study

English, speech, psychology, sociology, writing skills

Discover More

You can check out the social service field by volunteering at a food bank, an adult daycare center, a mental health institution, or a community center in your neighborhood.

Related Jobs

Social workers, clergy, occupational therapy assistants, physical therapy assistants, psychiatric and nursing aides, and recreation workers

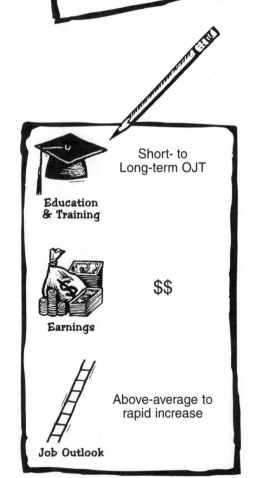

Education & Training
Short- to Long-term OJT

Earnings
$$

Job Outlook
Above-average to rapid increase

Social Workers

On the Job

Social workers work with people to help them find solutions to their problems. They might help a client find housing, a job, or health care. They deal with issues like child abuse, unplanned pregnancy, alcohol or drug abuse, and criminal behavior. They help people cope with serious illnesses and crisis situations. They may work in hospitals, social service agencies, group homes, government agencies, or schools.

Something Extra

Do people tell you you're a good listener? Do you enjoy helping your friends figure out solutions to their problems? Are you patient and good at puzzles? If so, social work might be a good field for you. A social worker's job is never the same from day to day. On Monday, you might help an elderly client find affordable housing, on Tuesday counsel a pregnant teenager, and on Wednesday visit an abused child in a foster home.

Subjects to Study

English, communication skills, psychology, biology, sociology, history, foreign languages

Discover More

Talk to the counselor at your school about this job. Ask about the training and the kinds of situations he or she deals with on a daily basis. Ask if he or she can help you set up a peer-counseling service.

Related Jobs

Clergy, counselors, psychologists, social and human service assistants, and special education teachers

Bachelor's degree to Master's degree

Education & Training

$$$–$$$$

Earnings

Above-average increase

Job Outlook

Protestant Ministers

On the Job

Protestant ministers help people in churches and communities. They write and give sermons, counsel people, and perform ceremonies such as baptisms, marriages, and funerals. Ministers are on call for emergencies 24 hours a day, seven days a week. Most spend four weekdays each week in the church office, plus Sundays at church. Some ministers teach in seminaries and colleges. Some ministers must move every few years.

Subjects to Study

English, writing skills, speech, social sciences, fine arts, music, foreign languages

Discover More

Call your local church and ask if you can help out in the church office after school. You might answer the phone, make copies, or help type the church newsletter. Spend time watching the minister work, and don't forget to ask a lot of questions!

Related Jobs

Social workers, psychologists, teachers, and counselors

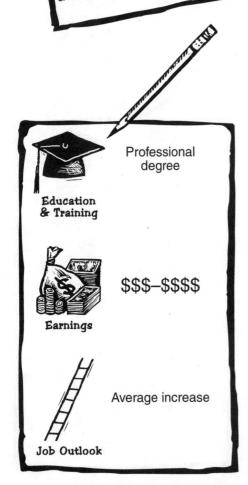

Education & Training
Professional degree

Earnings
$$$–$$$$

Job Outlook
Average increase

Rabbis

On the Job

Rabbis work in Jewish congregations, teaching Jewish law and tradition, counseling people, and conducting services such as weddings and funerals. They give sermons on the Sabbath and on Jewish holidays. Rabbis may be on call 24 hours a day, seven days a week. Some teach in seminaries and colleges or write for religious publications. Many rabbis participate in community activities.

Something Extra

Did you know there are three different branches of Judaism, and each ordains its own rabbis? In the United States, 41% of Jews are Reform, 40% are Conservative, and 7% are Orthodox. The rest are not affiliated with any branch. Some Orthodox groups do not even recognize that Reform and Conservative Jews are Jews at all.

Subjects to Study

English, writing skills, speech, social sciences, fine arts, music, foreign languages

Discover More

You can practice your public speaking skills by giving a talk to your class on something that interests you. Do some research to find information to back up your points. Can you hold your audience's attention?

Related Jobs

Social workers, psychologists, teachers, and counselors

Professional degree

Education & Training

$$$–$$$$

Earnings

Average increase

Job Outlook

Roman Catholic Priests

On the Job

Roman Catholic priests in local congregations write and give sermons, counsel people, and perform baptisms, weddings, and funerals. They may be on call 24 hours a day, seven days a week, and many live in parish rectories. All priests must take a vow of poverty and a vow never to marry. Priests also may be missionaries in foreign countries, live in monasteries, or teach in high schools, colleges, or seminaries.

Subjects to Study

English, speech, social studies, Latin, foreign languages, psychology, sociology, history

Discover More

Spend a day with your parish priest. What kinds of jobs does he do? Ask him about the hardest part of the job, and the most rewarding. He can tell you about the training you need to be a priest.

Related Jobs

Social workers, psychologists, teachers, and counselors

Education & Training — Professional degree

Earnings — $$

Job Outlook — Rapid increase

Adult Education Teachers

On the Job

Adult education teachers teach classes for people who want to update their job skills or prepare for the GED exam. They also teach writing, reading, and math to adults—often in evening or weekend classes. Others teach courses in flower arranging, cooking, or exercise to students who want to enrich their lives. Some work with adults who do not speak English.

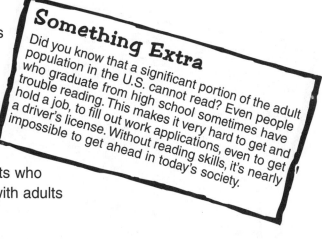

Something Extra

Did you know that a significant portion of the adult population in the U.S. cannot read? Even people who graduate from high school sometimes have trouble reading. This makes it very hard to get and hold a job, to fill out work applications, even to get a driver's license. Without reading skills, it's nearly impossible to get ahead in today's society.

Subjects to Study

English, communication and writing skills, math, psychology, biology, physics, chemistry, history, social sciences, physical education, home economics or shop courses, computer science, foreign languages

Discover More

Call a local community college or high school and ask for the catalog of continuing education courses. Find a class that interests you, then call the school and ask if you can sit in on a session of that class.

Related Jobs

Teachers, special education teachers, counselors, education administrators, public relations specialists, employment interviewers, and social workers

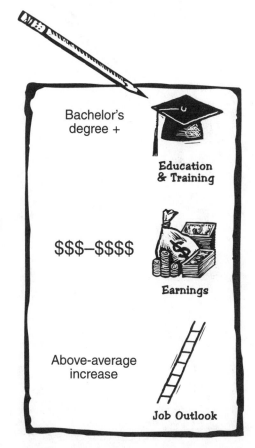

Bachelor's degree +

Education & Training

$$$–$$$$

Earnings

Above-average increase

Job Outlook

Archivists & Curators

On the Job

Archivists and curators choose, buy, and care for collections of books, records, art, and other items for libraries and museums. These items might be coins, stamps, plants, paintings, sculptures, or even animals. They may also work with records on paper, film, or computers. They plan exhibits, education programs, and tours. They work with the public and may travel to add to their collections.

Subjects to Study

English, speech, history, art, chemistry, physics, business, accounting

Discover More

Visit a museum or zoo in your area. Ask the tour guide about the collection. Who decides what to buy for the collection? Where do the exhibits come from? What would you like to see in the exhibit that's not already there?

Related Jobs

Anthropologists and archaeologists, botanists, genealogists, historians, librarians, artists, and teachers

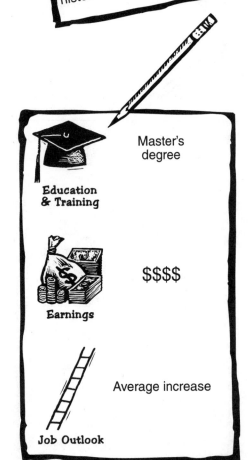

Education & Training
Master's degree

Earnings
$$$$

Job Outlook
Average increase

College & University Faculty

On the Job

College and university faculty teach at colleges, community colleges, universities, and research facilities. They specialize in one field, such as history, physics, or journalism. They do research and write articles and books about their findings. Most professors hold advanced degrees. While many schools do not hold classes during the summer months, faculty work year-round, preparing lectures, attending seminars, and conducting research.

Something Extra

Picture a university professor. Do you think of a white-bearded, bespectacled man lecturing in a big classroom? Well, that image is a bit outdated. Today's college and university faculty are young and old, men and women, of every ethnic and racial background. And they do more than lecture. Most are involved in some kind of original research in their field. If you love to learn about new ideas, this may be the job for you.

Subjects to Study

English, math, communication and writing skills, speech, sciences, social sciences, foreign languages, computer science

Discover More

Visit a college campus and attend a class or two. Watch the professor, and think about how the class resembles or differs from your classes at school. Talk to the professor after class and ask about the job.

Related Jobs

Elementary and secondary school teachers, librarians, writers, consultants, lobbyists, policy analysts, scientists, project managers, government and education administrators, counselors, and scientists

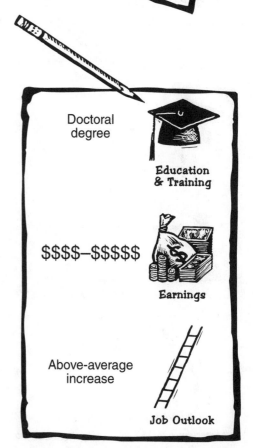

Doctoral degree

Education & Training

$$$$–$$$$$

Earnings

Above-average increase

Job Outlook

Counselors

Education & Training: Master's degree

Earnings: $$$$

Job Outlook: Little change

On the Job

Counselors help people with their problems; the work they do depends on the people they serve. *School counselors* help students with personal, social, and behavioral problems. *College placement counselors* help students decide on careers and find jobs. *Rehabilitation counselors* help people with disabilities and addictions. *Employment counselors* help people decide what kinds of jobs they want and help them find work.

Subjects to Study

English, speech, psychology, social studies, computer science, writing and communication skills

Discover More

Talk to your school counselor about this job. Find out what professional organizations he or she belongs to. Write to one of those organizations to learn more about counseling.

Related Jobs

Teachers, human resource professionals, human service workers, social workers, psychologists, psychiatrists, clergy, occupational therapists, and training and employment specialists

Librarians

On the Job

Librarians help people use the library and its materials. They help people find the books they need and fill out applications for library cards. They may give talks on how to use the library or read to children during special programs. Some manage other workers, prepare budgets, and order materials for their libraries. They may shelve books, update files, and design special displays.

Subjects to Study

English, literature, accounting, social sciences, business, psychology, computer science

Discover More

Take a tour of your school's library. Does your librarian order the books for your library? How does he or she decide which books to order? What guidelines does your school district provide? Ask if you can look through the publishers' catalogs and circle some titles that look interesting to you.

Related Jobs

Archivists and curators, publishers' representatives, research analysts, information brokers, and records managers

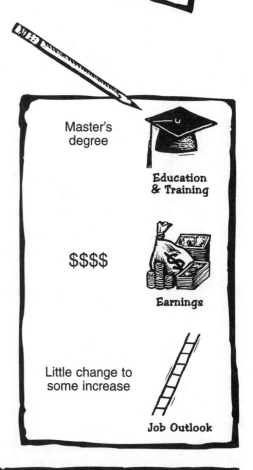

Master's degree

Education & Training

$$$$

Earnings

Little change to some increase

Job Outlook

Library Technicians

On the Job

Library technicians help librarians order, code, shelve, and organize library materials. They help people find materials and information. Some help maintain audiovisual equipment, prepare displays, and supervise other support staff. They answer questions, help patrons check out materials, and may send out notices to people with overdue books. Some work in school libraries, helping students find information they need for reports.

Subjects to Study

English, literature, accounting, computer skills, business courses

Discover More

Check your local library for volunteer opportunities. You might be put to work shelving books, helping at the check-out counter, supervising small children during reading programs, or straightening up at the end of the day.

Related Jobs

Library clerks, information clerks, record clerks, medical record technicians, museum technicians, teacher aides, legal assistants, and engineering and science technicians

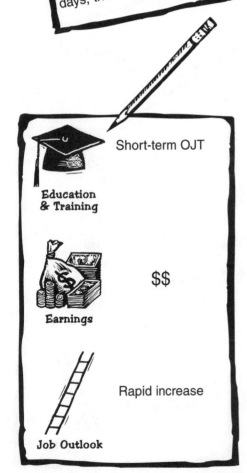

Short-term OJT

Education & Training

$$

Earnings

Rapid increase

Job Outlook

School Teachers—Kindergarten, Elementary, & Secondary

On the Job

Teachers help students learn in school. They plan lessons, prepare tests, grade papers, and write reports of students' progress. They meet with parents and school staff to talk about grades and problems. Some teach a specific grade; others teach one subject to students in many grades. Most work more than 40 hours a week. Some work second jobs during the summer months. Many supervise school activities such as clubs and sports teams.

Something Extra

Think about the challenges of being a working parent. You have to find someone to watch your kids while you are at work. This is hard enough during the school year, but in the summers and on Christmas break, it's especially tough. One of the things many teachers like about teaching is that they get the same days off as their kids. This cuts down on child-care costs, and lets them plan vacations and activities with their kids.

Subjects to Study

English, social studies, math, sciences, psychology, foreign languages, computer science

Discover More

Talk with your school counselor about programs such as peer tutoring or cadet teaching in your school. You can help younger students who are having trouble with a subject or grade papers for a teacher.

Related Jobs

College and university faculty, counselors, education administrators, employment interviewers, librarians, preschool workers, social workers, trainers, and employee development specialists

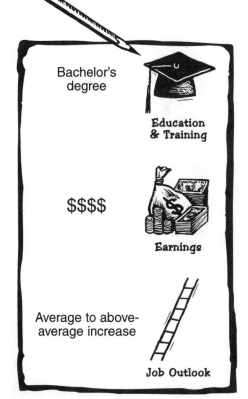

Bachelor's degree

Education & Training

$$$$

Earnings

Average to above-average increase

Job Outlook

Special Education Teachers

On the Job

Special education teachers work with students who have disabilities. Most work in elementary, middle, or high schools, but some work with toddlers and preschoolers. They prepare classes to meet their students' needs, grade papers, and write reports. They may teach academic studies or life skills. They meet with parents, counselors, school psychologists, and occupational or physical therapists to come up with the best school plan for each student.

Subjects to Study

English, social studies, math, sciences, psychology, foreign languages, computer science

Discover More

Arrange with your teacher to spend a day observing a special education class at your school. Watch how the teacher interacts with the students. You might be able to help out by reading to younger children or tutoring them.

Related Jobs

School teachers, counselors, psychologists, social workers, speech pathologists, and occupational, physical, and recreational therapists

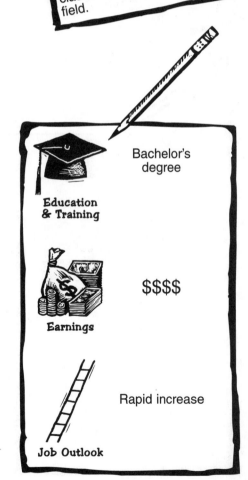

Education & Training
Bachelor's degree

Earnings
$$$$

Job Outlook
Rapid increase

Chiropractors

On the Job

Chiropractors help people who have problems with their muscles, nerves, or skeleton, especially the spine. They examine patients, order tests, and take X rays. They treat patients by massaging or adjusting the spinal column. They also use water and heat therapy. They stress nutrition, exercise, and reducing stress in treatment. They do not prescribe drugs or perform surgery. Many are self-employed.

Something Extra

What does a chiropractor have to do with treating headaches? As it turns out, quite a lot. Headaches can result from poor posture, tension, or a misalignment of the spinal cord. Using massage, heat therapy, and realignment exercises and techniques, chiropractors can help people who suffer from persistent or chronic headaches. They also teach people how to prevent headaches in the first place, which may be the best treatment of all.

Subjects to Study

Health, biology, anatomy, nutrition, chemistry, physics, psychology, math, social sciences

Discover More

Aromatherapy is the practice of using different smells to relax, calm, or energize yourself. Try an experiment at home. Buy several different scented candles. Each evening at dinner, light a different candle. (Get your parents' permission first!) How do the different scents affect your mood?

Related Jobs

Physicians, dentists, optometrists, podiatrists, veterinarians, occupational therapists, and physical therapists

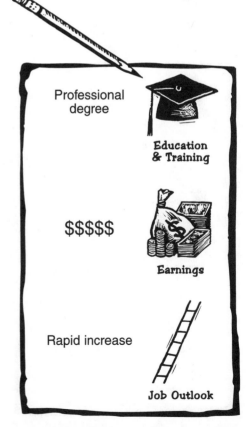

Professional degree

Education & Training

$$$$$

Earnings

Rapid increase

Job Outlook

Dentists

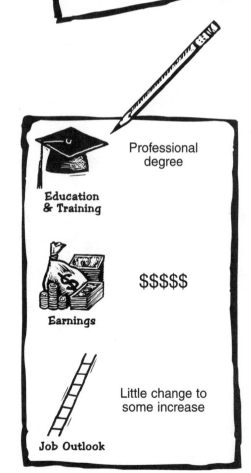

Something Extra

Dentists have been practicing for nearly 7,000 years, although you might not recognize some of the treatments used back then as dentistry. In ancient Babylon, for example, "dentists" used worms, prayers, and herbs to treat tooth decay. In the Middle Ages, dentists were considered the first surgeons—although about all they could do was remove teeth, which they did to treat nearly every condition you can think of.

Education & Training
Professional degree

Earnings
$$$$$

Job Outlook
Little change to some increase

On the Job

Dentists help people take care of their teeth. They remove teeth and straighten them with braces, repair broken teeth, and fill cavities. They may replace a patient's original teeth with a "bridge" of false teeth. They may also perform surgery to treat gum disease. They teach people how to brush, floss, and care for their teeth to prevent problems. They wear masks, gloves, and safety glasses to protect themselves from infectious diseases. Many are self-employed.

Subjects to Study

Biology, anatomy, chemistry, physics, health, business math, communication skills

Discover More

Visit your dentist and ask him or her about the job. What kind of training is available in your area? What is the best part of the job? What's the worst? Is you dentist bothered that so many people are afraid of him or her?

Related Jobs

Clinical psychologists, optometrists, physicians, chiropractors, veterinarians, and podiatrists

Optometrists

On the Job

Optometrists examine people's eyes to diagnose vision problems and eye diseases. They prescribe glasses and contact lenses and treat certain eye diseases. Some optometrists work especially with the elderly or children. Others develop ways to protect workers' eyes from on-the-job strain or injury. Many are self-employed and work Saturdays and evenings to meet their patients' schedules.

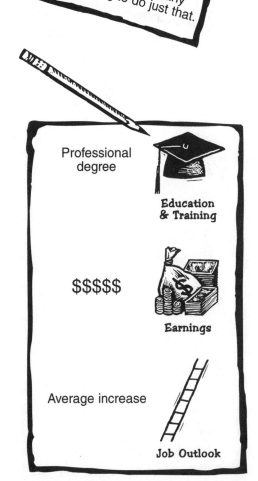

Something Extra

Retinopathy of Prematurity (ROP) is the leading cause of blindness in children today. It is caused when babies are born too early and their retinas have not had time to develop properly. Yet the major cause of ROP is completely preventable: Fluorescent lighting in hospital nurseries can damage sensitive infant eyes in a matter of minutes. Dimming the lights can prevent ROP in many cases, and hospitals are beginning to do just that.

Subjects to Study

Physics, chemistry, biology, anatomy, psychology, speech, business math

Discover More

Arrange for your class to have a vision screening. With your teacher, contact a local optometrist and ask him or her to visit your school, talk about the job, and do a basic vision screening.

Related Jobs

Chiropractors, dentists, physicians, podiatrists, veterinarians, speech-language pathologists, and audiologists

Professional degree

Education & Training

$$$$$

Earnings

Average increase

Job Outlook

Physicians

On the Job

Physicians help people who are sick or have been hurt. They examine patients, perform tests, prescribe treatments, and teach people about health care. Doctors specialize in one area, such as family practice, surgery, or pregnancy and baby care. They work in hospitals, clinics, and in private practice. Many work 60 hours a week or more. They may be on call for emergency visits to the hospital. Most doctors must travel frequently from their offices to hospitals to care for patients.

Subjects to Study

Physics, chemistry, biology, psychology, health, nutrition, English, math

Discover More

Call your local hospital and ask about volunteer opportunities. Many have programs that let young people visit with or read to patients, deliver things, greet visitors, and help with the library cart.

Related Jobs

Acupuncturists, audiologists, chiropractors, dentists, optometrists, podiatrists, speech pathologists, and veterinarians

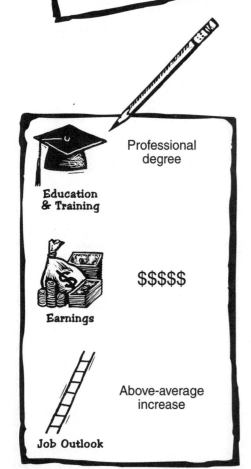

Education & Training
Professional degree

Earnings
$$$$$

Job Outlook
Above-average increase

Podiatrists

On the Job

Podiatrists diagnose and treat diseases and injuries of the foot and lower leg. They may treat corns, calluses, ingrown toenails, bunions, heel spurs, and arch problems. They also treat ankle and foot injuries, deformities, and infections. They take care of foot problems caused by diseases such as diabetes. They prescribe medications and order physical therapy. They set broken bones and perform surgery. Podiatrists usually run their own small businesses.

Something Extra

Did you know that one in four Americans has foot problems? And women are four times as likely as men to have serious foot problems! The culprit? Those beautiful, elegant high-heeled shoes. That's why the American Association of Podiatrists recommends that women wear high heels only occasionally. For everyday wear, the doctors recommend sensible, wide-toed, flat shoes or tennis shoes.

Subjects to Study

Biology, chemistry, physics, anatomy, health, English, business math

Discover More

For more information on this job, write to the American Podiatric Medical Association, 9312 Old Georgetown Rd., Bethesda, MD 20814-1621.

Related Jobs

Chiropractors, dentists, optometrists, physicians, and veterinarians

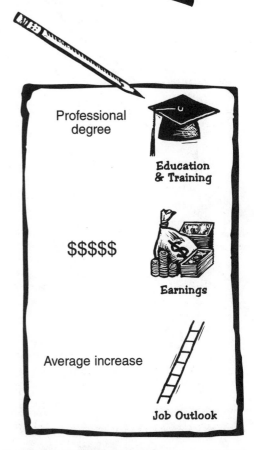

Professional degree

Education & Training

$$$$$

Earnings

Average increase

Job Outlook

Veterinarians

On the Job

Veterinarians care for pets, farm animals, zoo residents, and laboratory animals. They set broken bones, treat injuries, prescribe medicine, perform surgery, and vaccinate animals against diseases. They teach people how to care for animals. Most veterinarians treat animals in private clinics or hospitals and work 50 hours or more a week. They may work nights and weekends. A number of veterinarians engage in research.

Subjects to Study

Biology, chemistry, physics, business math, English

Discover More

Visit an animal shelter and talk to the workers about volunteer opportunities. Some shelters let volunteers come in to feed, bathe, and pet the animals.

Related Jobs

Chiropractors, physicians, podiatrists, animal trainers, zoologists, farmers, and marine biologists

Education & Training
Professional degree

Earnings
$$$$–$$$$$

Job Outlook
Above-average increase

Dietitians & Nutritionists

On the Job

Dietitians and nutritionists plan, prepare, and serve meals in clinics, schools, nursing homes, and hospitals. They help prevent and treat illnesses by teaching clients to eat properly. Some specialize in helping overweight or critically ill patients, or in caring for kidney or diabetic patients. Those supervising kitchen workers may be on their feet most of the day in a hot, steamy kitchen.

Something Extra

What is your favorite food? Is it a healthy, low-fat salad, or a big, greasy burger with fries? The food we eat affects our lives in countless ways. Bad eating habits can lead to obesity, low energy and fatigue, diabetes, heart disease, and certain kinds of cancer.

Start today on a new, healthy lifestyle by watching what you put into your mouth. Learning to eat healthy foods now will make a huge difference in your life today, and tomorrow.

Subjects to Study

Health, nutrition, home economics, biology, chemistry, English, accounting

Discover More

Plan and prepare a healthy, low-fat meal for your family. Be sure to include grains, fruits, vegetables, dairy products, and protein.

Related Jobs

Home economists, food service managers, nurses, and health educators

Bachelor's degree

Education & Training

$$$$

Earnings

Above-average increase

Job Outlook

Occupational Therapists

On the Job

Occupational therapists help people with disabilities become independent and productive. They may help a patient learn to use a wheelchair or work on a new skill. They also help patients find jobs and develop job skills. They usually work in hospitals, schools, or rehab centers. Some provide home health care. Most spend a lot of time on their feet. The job can be tiring, because therapists must sometimes lift patients and move equipment.

Subjects to Study

Biology, chemistry, physics, health, art, psychology, English, foreign languages

Discover More

Volunteer at a local nursing home to help with activities. You might teach a stroke victim to knit, read to a person whose sight is fading, or simply visit someone whose family is far away.

Related Jobs

Physical therapists, chiropractors, speech pathologists and audiologists, rehabilitation counselors, and recreational therapists

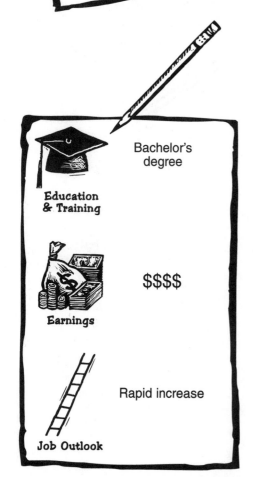

Bachelor's degree

Education & Training

$$$$

Earnings

Rapid increase

Job Outlook

Pharmacists

On the Job

Pharmacists measure and sell medication to people who are sick when a doctor says they need it. They must know about the correct use, makeup, and effects of drugs. They tell patients about medicines, including reactions and possible side effects, and answer questions. Those in hospitals and clinics advise doctors and nurses on drugs and their effects. Most pharmacists spend much of the workday on their feet. They may wear gloves and safety masks when working with drugs. Many work nights and weekends.

Something Extra

A big part of a pharmacist's job is answering questions. Because pharmacists work with the public, these might range from "Can I take this cold remedy with this pain reliever?" to "Where's the bathroom?"

Their special knowledge makes them the expert for patients and doctors alike. In fact, several cases have been reported of pharmacists catching doctors' errors, especially in hospitals, often with life-saving effects. Maybe instead of white lab coats, they should wear white hats!

Subjects to Study

Math, biology, chemistry, physics, social sciences, English, foreign languages

Discover More

Talk to a pharmacist and ask about the training needed for this job. Ask how he or she keeps up with new drugs that hit the market every day. Then, just for fun, ask about the most ridiculous question he or she has been asked.

Related Jobs

Chemists, medical assistants, and pharmacologists

Bachelor's degree

Education & Training

$$$$$

Earnings

Average increase

Job Outlook

Physical Therapists

On the Job

Physical therapists work with accident victims, stroke patients, and people with disabilities. They evaluate patients and make plans to help them recover their physical abilities and relieve pain. They may use electricity, heat, or cold to relieve pain, reduce swelling, or increase flexibility. They work in hospitals, clinics, and private offices with special equipment. Physical therapists must be strong enough to move patients and equipment.

Subjects to Study

Biology, chemistry, physics, psychology, anatomy, English, foreign languages

Discover More

Talk to the gym teacher at your school about this kind of work. Ask him or her to help you put together an exercise plan to help you build your own strength and endurance.

Related Jobs

Occupational therapists, recreational therapists, speech pathologists and audiologists, respiratory therapists, chiropractors, acupuncturists, and athletic trainers

Education & Training

Bachelor's degree

Earnings

$$$$–$$$$$

Job Outlook

Rapid increase

Physician Assistants

On the Job

Physician assistants always work under the supervision of a physician. They handle many of the routine but time-consuming tasks physicians do, such as taking medical records, examining patients, and ordering X rays and tests. They also treat minor injuries. They often work weekends and evenings. Physician assistants may be on their feet for long periods of time.

Something Extra

In many small, rural communities in the United States, medical doctors are in short supply. Some communities have no resident doctors at all. In such communities, physician assistants (PAs) are the primary health care providers. They see patients on a day-to-day basis, handling routine office visits, while a doctor visits the clinic one or two days a week. The PA can call the doctor for advice or in emergencies.

Subjects to Study

Biology, chemistry, math, psychology, English, foreign languages, anatomy, nutrition

Discover More

To learn more about this job, send for a free brochure, Physicians Assistants—Partners in Medicine, from the American Academy of Physician Assistants, 950 North Washington St., Alexandria, VA 22314.

Related Jobs

Nurse practitioners, physical therapists, occupational therapists, clinical psychologists, and speech and hearing clinicians

Bachelor's degree

Education & Training

$$$$

Earnings

Rapid increase

Job Outlook

Recreational Therapists

On the Job

Recreational therapists help people with medical problems improve their health and well-being. They teach patients games, arts and crafts, dance, music, and sports activities. These activities help patients regain skills they've lost because of illness or injury and improve their state of mind. They work closely with medical staff in hospitals and nursing homes. They must be strong enough to move patients and equipment and to participate in activities.

Subjects to Study

English, speech, communication skills, anatomy, psychology, health, art, music, dance, physical education

Discover More

Volunteer some time each week at a nursing home in your neighborhood. Ask the activity director if you can help him or her plan and carry out activities for the residents. You might help with an art project, read to a patient, or just play along in a game.

Related Jobs

Occupational therapists, counselors, medical assistants, and rehabilitation therapists

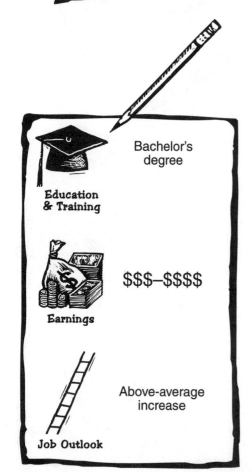

Education & Training
Bachelor's degree

Earnings
$$$–$$$$

Job Outlook
Above-average increase

Registered Nurses

On the Job

Registered nurses care for the sick and injured and help people stay well. In clinics, hospitals, and nursing homes, they provide much of the day-to-day care for patients, under a doctor's supervision. They take patient histories, give shots and medicines, and teach patients about helping with their own care. Some assist in surgeries. Nurses often work nights, weekends, and holidays. They must be able to cope with emergencies and high stress.

Something Extra

You might know that nurses help doctors, but did you know that if you have surgery, your life might depend on one? According to several studies, hospitals with more registered nurses have lower death rates following surgeries than those with fewer nurses.
That's because it's often a nurse who notices if a patient has a bad reaction to a drug, complications from surgery, or another problem. So it's nurses who often save lives.

Subjects to Study

Health, biology, chemistry, physics, anatomy, psychology, nutrition, English, foreign languages

Discover More

One of the best ways to learn about working in the medical field is to volunteer at a hospital or nursing home. You might organize activities, visit with patients, deliver supplies, or help with basic patient care.

Related Jobs

Occupational therapists, paramedics, physical therapists, physician assistants, and respiratory therapists

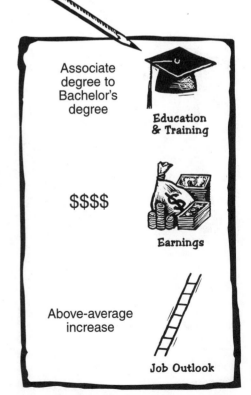

Associate degree to Bachelor's degree

Education & Training

$$$$

Earnings

Above-average increase

Job Outlook

Respiratory Therapists

On the Job

Respiratory therapists care for patients with breathing problems, from premature babies to heart attack victims. They perform tests, connect patients to machines that help in breathing, and teach patients how to use these machines at home. Therapists may also help in surgery by removing mucus from a patient's lungs so he or she can breathe more easily. Those in hospitals spend most of their time on their feet. They must be able to work calmly in emergencies.

Subjects to Study

Health, biology, chemistry, physics, English

Discover More

Asthma is on the rise in the United States, especially among children. Talk to someone who has asthma and find out what type of medicine or therapy he or she uses in an asthma attack.

Related Jobs

Dialysis technicians, registered nurses, occupational therapists, physical therapists, and radiation therapy technologists

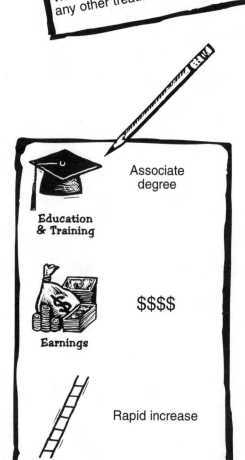

Education & Training
Associate degree

Earnings
$$$$

Job Outlook
Rapid increase

Speech-Language Pathologists & Audiologists

On the Job

Speech-language pathologists work with people who cannot speak well. They teach patients how to improve their language skills. They may teach sign language to nonspeaking patients. Audiologists work with people who cannot hear. They recommend treatments such as hearing aids, implants, or surgery. They work in hospitals, nursing homes, and schools.

Something Extra

It used to be that deaf people were consigned to lives on the sidelines, but not today. Heather Whitestone, Miss America of 1995, is deaf. She communicates through speaking and dancing and lives quite successfully in a hearing world. Deaf actress Marlee Matlin won an Academy Award for her role in the movie *Children of a Lesser God* and played a successful district attorney in the hit TV series "Reasonable Doubt."

Subjects to Study

English, foreign languages, speech, biology, chemistry, physics, psychology

Discover More

Speech therapists help clients learn to speak clearly. Practice your speaking skills by tape recording yourself while reading. Play the tape back and listen to your speaking skills. Are you clear and understandable? If not, practice speaking in front of a mirror and watch how you make the sounds.

Related Jobs

Occupational therapists, physical therapists, recreational therapists, and rehabilitation counselors

Master's degree

Education & Training

$$$$

Earnings

Rapid increase

Job Outlook

Cardiovascular Technologists & Technicians

On the Job

Cardiovascular technologists and technicians help doctors treat heart and blood vessel diseases. They use a variety of tests, monitor the results, and prepare patients for tests. They may schedule patient appointments, type doctors' reports, keep patient files, and care for the testing equipment. They usually work in hospitals and clinics and may work evenings and weekends.

Subjects to Study

Shop courses, communication skills, math, computer skills, health

Discover More

Talk to an EKG supervisor or a cardiologist at your local hospital. Ask a technician about on-the-job training in your area. The hospital staff can tell you more about this job.

Related Jobs

Radiologic technologists, diagnostic medical sonographers, electroencephalographic technologists, and respiratory therapists

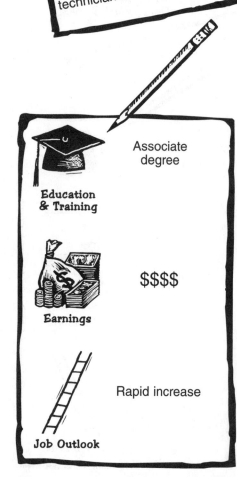

Associate degree

Education & Training

$$$$

Earnings

Rapid increase

Job Outlook

Clinical Laboratory Technologists & Technicians

On the Job

These workers do medical tests to help detect, diagnose, and treat diseases. They match blood types, test for drug levels, and look for abnormal cells. They analyze test results and send them back to doctors. Special equipment allows them to do more than one test at a time. They may work nights and weekends. They wear gloves and masks to protect themselves from infectious specimens.

Something Extra

Cancer is a deadly disease, but today's screening tests are helping doctors win the war against this killer. Pap smears detect cervical cancer, mammograms find breast cancer, and biopsies help determine if suspicious tissues are cancerous or not. After the doctor administers the test, he or she sends the results to a lab for analysis. It is the lab technician who tests the samples and decides if they are cancerous. These workers are in the business of saving lives.

Subjects to Study

Biology, chemistry, physics, computer skills, math

Discover More

Rub slices of white bread against different surfaces: a trash can, your hair, the inside of your desk, the floor, dirt, whatever. Seal each piece in a plastic bag with a label telling what it touched. Let the bags sit for a week, then look at them through a magnifying glass. Which surface generated the most mold? (Important: Throw the bags away without opening them. Mold can make you sick!)

Related Jobs

Chemists, science technicians, crime laboratory analysts, and veterinary laboratory technicians

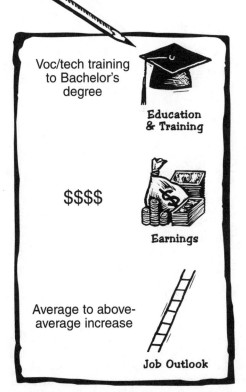

Voc/tech training to Bachelor's degree

Education & Training

$$$$

Earnings

Average to above-average increase

Job Outlook

Dental Hygienists

On the Job

Dental hygienists examine patients' teeth and gums to find disease. They help dentists by cleaning patients' teeth, taking and developing X rays, and applying fluoride to the teeth. They teach patients how to brush and floss their teeth correctly. Many work part-time for more than one dentist, and they often work on weekends and evenings. They wear gloves and masks to protect themselves from diseases.

Subjects to Study

Biology, chemistry, health, nutrition, anatomy, English, foreign languages

Discover More

Do a simple experiment in your class. Have half the students brush their teeth three times a day and floss every day. Ask the other half to continue with a regular teeth-cleaning routine. At the end of the school year, invite a dentist to check the class's teeth. Which group has better checkups?

Related Jobs

Dental assistants, ophthalmic medical assistants, office nurses, medical assistants, and physician assistants

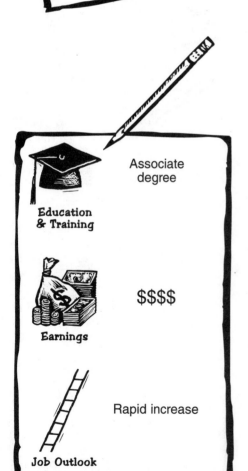

Education & Training
Associate degree

Earnings
$$$$

Job Outlook
Rapid increase

Dispensing Opticians

On the Job

Dispensing opticians work for eye doctors, making glasses and contact lenses according to the doctors' orders. They also keep customer records, track inventory, and help customers find frames that fit them well. Many work evenings and weekends or part-time. They must be careful with the glass-cutting machinery and chemicals they use to make lenses.

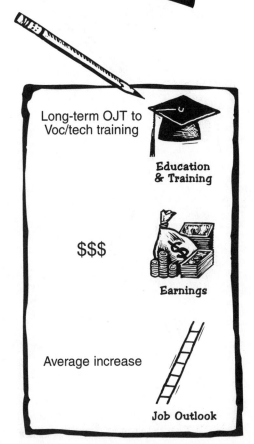

Something Extra

When was the first eye surgery performed? Would you guess this century? Or in the 1800s? How about in 1000 B.C.? That's right, long before glasses were invented, ancient surgeons were removing cataracts from people's eyes. We have evidence that this surgery was being performed in India more than 3,000 years ago—probably without anesthesia!

Subjects to Study

Physics, anatomy, algebra, geometry, mechanical drawing, business math

Discover More

Visit an optical store in your community. Look through the wide selection of eyewear and decide which frames best fit your face. Talk to one of the dispensing opticians about this job.

Related Jobs

Jewelers, ophthalmic laboratory technicians, dental laboratory technicians, prosthetics technicians, camera repairers, and watch repairers

Long-term OJT to Voc/tech training

Education & Training

$$$

Earnings

Average increase

Job Outlook

EEG Technologists

On the Job

EEG technologists use a special machine to record brain waves for doctors. Doctors use the results of these tests to find brain tumors, help stroke victims, and make other medical decisions. Sometimes EEG results are used to determine brain activity in coma patients. EEG technologists must be strong enough to lift patients who are very ill. Most work normal hours, although they may be on call for emergencies.

Subjects to Study

Health, biology, math, shop courses, computer science, English

Discover More

Your brain is like a computer. Learn more about it by checking your library for books and videos about the "control room" of your body. Find out if you are a left-brained or right-brained person.

Related Jobs

Radiologic technologists, nuclear medicine technologists, perfusionists, and EKG technologists

Education & Training
Long-term OJT

Earnings
$$$$

Job Outlook
Above-average to rapid increase

Emergency Medical Technicians

On the Job

Emergency medical technicians (EMTs) drive ambulances and give emergency medical care. They determine a patient's medical condition at the scene, stabilize the patient, then drive him or her to the hospital. They work outdoors in all kinds of weather, and the work can be very stressful. Some patients may become violent, and EMTs may be exposed to diseases. They work for fire departments, hospitals, and private ambulance services.

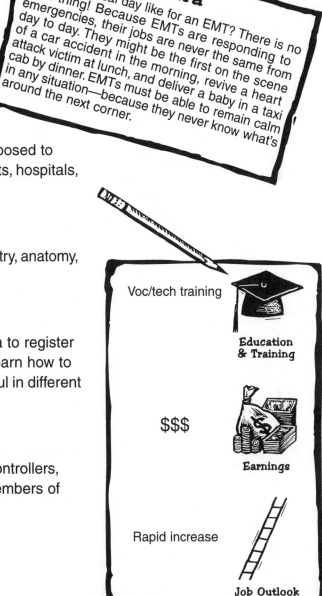

Something Extra

What's a typical day like for an EMT? There is no such thing! Because EMTs are responding to emergencies, their jobs are never the same from day to day. They might be the first on the scene of a car accident in the morning, revive a heart attack victim at lunch, and deliver a baby in a taxi cab by dinner. EMTs must be able to remain calm in any situation—because they never know what's around the next corner.

Subjects to Study

Driver education, health, biology, chemistry, anatomy, English, foreign languages

Discover More

Check with the Red Cross in your area to register for a first aid or CPR course. You can learn how to save another person's life and be helpful in different kinds of emergencies.

Related Jobs

Police officers, firefighters, air traffic controllers, workers in health occupations, and members of the Air Force

Voc/tech training

Education & Training

$$$

Earnings

Rapid increase

Job Outlook

Health Information Technicians

On the Job

These workers organize and keep track of patients' medical records. First, they make sure all the right forms have been signed. Then, they put the information into a computer file. Finally, they code the information, so it can be pulled up easily. They may work day, evening, or night shifts. Health information technicians must be computer literate and pay attention to details.

Subjects to Study

English, computer skills, anatomy, biology

Discover More

The American Health Information Management Association offers an independent study program for health information technicians. You can write to the association at 919 N. Michigan Ave., Suite 1400, Chicago, IL 60611.

Related Jobs

Medical secretaries, medical transcribers, medical writers, and medical illustrators

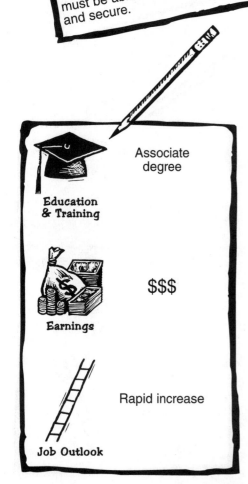

Education & Training — Associate degree

Earnings — $$$

Job Outlook — Rapid increase

Licensed Practical Nurses

On the Job

Licensed practical nurses (LPNs) take care of sick and injured people. They are supervised by doctors or registered nurses. They help patients with bathing, dressing, and personal hygiene, feed them, and care for their emotional needs. They keep their patients as comfortable as possible. Some LPNs help deliver, care for, and feed infants. They may work nights, weekends, and holidays. LPNs must be strong enough to lift patients and able to deal with stress. They can be exposed to infectious diseases.

Something Extra

Some LPNs work as private-duty nurses. Instead of working for a hospital or clinic, these nurses provide in-home care to patients. They may work 8 to 12 hours a day caring for a single patient. In some cases, their duties involve caring for other members of the patient's family as well. At night, most return to their own homes and families, but some actually live with their patients' families while they provide care.

Subjects to Study

Health, anatomy, psychology, first aid, nutrition, home economics courses, English, foreign languages

Discover More

Licensed practical nursing courses are offered in some high school vocational programs. Talk to your school counselor about these programs and find out if any are available through high schools in your area.

Related Jobs

Emergency medical technicians, social service aides, human service workers, and teacher aides

Voc/tech training

Education & Training

$$$

Earnings

Above-average increase

Job Outlook

Nuclear Medicine Technologists

On the Job

Nuclear medicine technologists give radioactive drugs to patients. These drugs help doctors diagnose and treat diseases. Using a camera, the technologist follows the drug as it enters the patient's body and records the drug's effects. Technologists must keep accurate, detailed patient records. Technologists must be careful to keep from being exposed to too much radiation. They wear badges that measure radiation levels.

Subjects to Study

Biology, chemistry, physics, math, computer science

Discover More

You can get more information about this job by writing to the Joint Review Committee on Educational Programs in Nuclear Medicine Technology, #1 2nd Avenue East, Suite C, Polson, MT 59860-2320.

Related Jobs

Radiologic technologists, diagnostic medical sonographers, cardiology technologists, EEG technologists, clinical laboratory technologists, perfusionists, and respiratory therapists

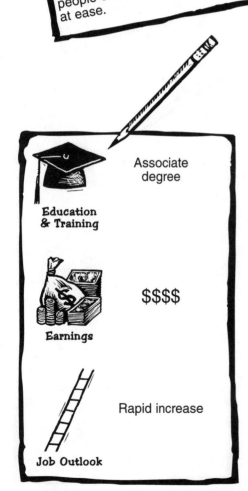

Education & Training
Associate degree

Earnings
$$$$

Job Outlook
Rapid increase

Radiologic Technologists

On the Job

Radiologic technologists work in hospitals and clinics. They operate the machines that take X ray pictures or magnetic resolution pictures of people's bones and internal organs. They must wear badges that measure the amount of radiation they are exposed to on the job. Radiologic technologists may work nights or weekends and may be on call during odd hours. They are on their feet most of the day and must be strong enough to lift patients.

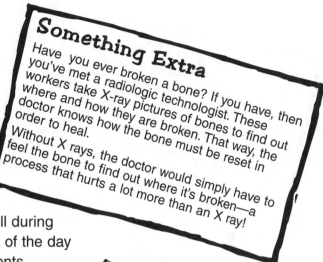

Something Extra

Have you ever broken a bone? If you have, then you've met a radiologic technologist. These workers take X-ray pictures of bones to find out where and how they are broken. That way, the doctor knows how the bone must be reset in order to heal.

Without X rays, the doctor would simply have to feel the bone to find out where it's broken—a process that hurts a lot more than an X ray!

Subjects to Study

Biology, chemistry, physics, math, computer science

Discover More

You can get more information about this job by writing to the Joint Review Committee on Educational Programs in Nuclear Medicine Technology, #1 2nd Avenue East, Suite C, Polson, MT 59860-2320.

Related Jobs

Nuclear medicine technologists, diagnostic medical sonographers, cardiology technologists, EEG technologists, clinical laboratory technologists, perfusionists, and respiratory therapists

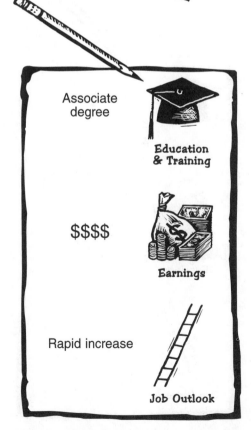

Associate degree

Education & Training

$$$$

Earnings

Rapid increase

Job Outlook

Surgical Technicians

On the Job

Surgical technologists set up equipment in the operating room, prepare patients for surgery, and take patients to and from the operating room. They help the surgical team "scrub" and put on gloves, masks, and surgical clothing. During an operation, they help with supplies and instruments and operate lights and equipment. After the operation, they restock the operating room. Surgical technicians must be able to stay calm and steady in stressful circumstances.

Subjects to Study

Health, biology, chemistry, math, anatomy, English, foreign languages

Discover More

Surgical technicians must be comfortable dealing with operations of all kinds. One way to test your tolerance for this is to take a biology course in which you dissect an animal.

Related Jobs

Licensed practical nurses, respiratory therapists, medical laboratory assistants, medical assistants, dental assistants, and physical therapy aides

Education & Training
Voc/tech training

Earnings
$$$–$$$$

Job Outlook
Rapid increase

Broadcast Technicians

On the Job

Broadcast technicians work with electronic equipment to record and transmit radio and television programs. They operate, install, and repair microphones, TV cameras, tape recorders, and antennas. They often work holidays, weekends, and evenings for news programs. When disasters happen, they must be on the scene to record the news. Setting up equipment sometimes requires heavy lifting and climbing.

Something Extra

Did you ever wonder how a movie-maker got a certain sound—maybe the hum of a spacecraft engine or the blast of a star exploding? The sound track in a movie is made by sound mixers. Using a process called *dubbing*, sound mixers sit at a console facing the movie screen and add the special-effect sounds and music. The sounds are then "mixed" on one master tape, which becomes the movie's sound track.

Subjects to Study

Math, shop courses, physics, electronics, English, computer skills

Discover More

Build your own electronic equipment using a hobby kit. Check a toy or hobby store to see what kind of equipment is available. Operating a "ham" or amateur radio is great experience for this occupation.

Related Jobs

Drafters, engineering and science technicians, surveyors, air traffic controllers, respiratory therapists, EEG technicians, and medical laboratory technicians

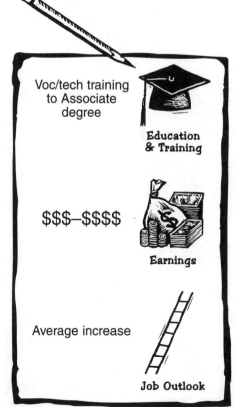

Voc/tech training to Associate degree

Education & Training

$$$–$$$$

Earnings

Average increase

Job Outlook

Public Relations Specialists

On the Job

Public relations specialists work to present a good image of their clients to the public. Their job is to make sure the clients' good news is spread far and wide, and to put a positive "spin" on bad news. They write press releases and speeches and set up "photo opportunities" of their clients doing good things. Many work more than 40 hours a week. In an emergency, they may be on call around the clock.

Subjects to Study

English, creative writing, journalism, psychology, sociology, computer skills, public speaking, foreign languages

Discover More

Write a press release for your class, announcing some good news or interesting event. Be sure the release is honest but puts forth the best possible image. Keep it short and snappy, to be sure it gets attention!

Related Jobs

Fund raisers, lobbyists, promotion managers, advertising managers, and police officers involved in community relations

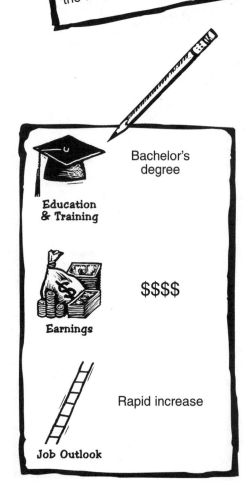

Education & Training
Bachelor's degree

Earnings
$$$$

Job Outlook
Rapid increase

Radio & Television Announcers & Newscasters

On the Job

Radio announcers (or disc jockeys) plan and perform radio programs. They may choose and play music, interview guests, and write program material. Television announcers and newscasters prepare and present the news, weather, and sports, although most specialize in one of these areas. They may work unusual hours, including very early in the morning and very late at night. When emergency situations arise, they must be there to cover them for the news.

Subjects to Study

English, public speaking, drama, foreign languages, electronics, computer skills

Discover More

Ask the principal at your school if you can make the morning announcements one day. Write out your "intro" and try to make it humorous or catchy. Can you entertain your audience members while you keep them informed? That's the job of a news anchor.

Related Jobs

Interpreters, sales workers, public relations specialists, teachers, and actors

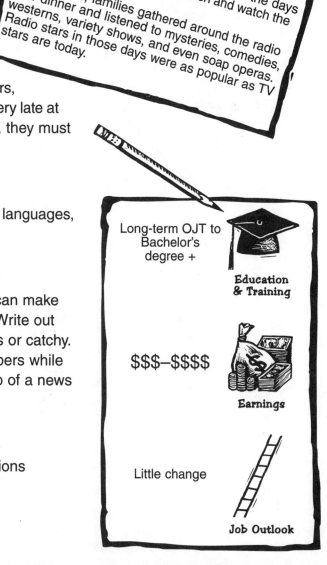

Something Extra

What did people do before television—in the days when you couldn't just flip a switch and watch the tube?

In the 1940s, families gathered around the radio after dinner and listened to mysteries, comedies, westerns, variety shows, and even soap operas. Radio stars in those days were as popular as TV stars are today.

Long-term OJT to Bachelor's degree +

Education & Training

$$$–$$$$

Earnings

Little change

Job Outlook

Reporters & Correspondents

Something Extra

Yellow journalism means writing about sensational events in order to sell more newspapers. For example, a newspaper might focus on a famous murder trial and the people involved. The term comes from the yellow ink used in a comic strip called "The Yellow Kid."

Today, we use the term *tabloid journalism* to describe the same thing. Some critics say that even mainstream newspapers engage in tabloid journalism these days.

On the Job

Reporters and correspondents gather information and write articles about events around the world. Some take photographs or shoot videos. Radio and television reporters often report "live" from the scene of crimes or disasters. The work is usually hectic and stressful, and the deadlines are tight. Reporting can be dangerous work and requires long hours, irregular schedules, and travel.

Subjects to Study

English, journalism, social studies, history, creative writing, speech, computer science, foreign languages

Discover More

Collect three or more newspapers that are all reporting the same story. Read the reports, then make notes about how each paper's story differs from the others. The facts may be the same, but one paper may choose to play up sensational aspects while another pushes a different viewpoint.

Related Jobs

Technical writers, copy writers, public relations workers, educational writers, biographers, fiction and screen writers, and editors

Education & Training
Bachelor's degree

Earnings
$$$–$$$$

Job Outlook
Little change

Writers & Editors

On the Job

Writers write novels and nonfiction books, articles, movies, plays, poems, and ads. They do research to find material, and they spend a lot of time revising and rewriting. They must also be able to sell what they have written. Editors choose the stories and books that publishing houses will print. Magazine editors choose articles for publication and assign stories to writers. Many of them also write stories and articles. Editors also review, rewrite, and correct the work of writers.

Something Extra

So you want to be a writer, but you can't find time to write? Next time you feel that way, consider Anthony Trollope. This English novelist in the 1800s worked full-time at the post office, yet managed to write dozens of books that are still in print today. How did he find the time? He wrote by the clock—producing a set number of pages every day. Trollope once wrote, "Three hours a day will produce as much as a man ought to write." Now, what was your excuse for not writing?

Subjects to Study

English, creative writing, journalism, computer skills, history, psychology, business math

Discover More

Submit a story to a local newspaper or magazine. Check out the *Writer's Market* for those that encourage young writers. Enter a writing contest.

Related Jobs

Newspaper reporters and correspondents, radio and television announcers, advertising and public relations workers, and teachers

Bachelor's degree

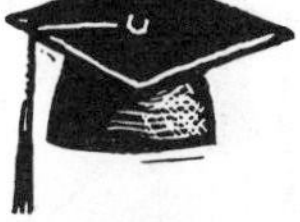

Education & Training

$$$$

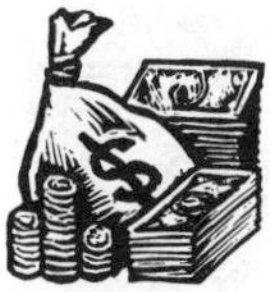

Earnings

Little change

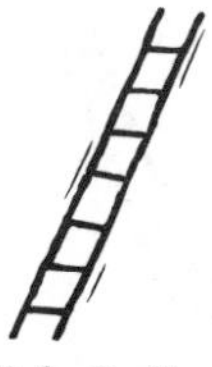

Job Outlook

Designers

On the Job

Designers create things that are attractive and useful. They may design clothing, furniture, homes, cars, flowers, or new products for the home or office. They must decide what materials to use and consider fashion trends, safety, and cost. Designers work in all kinds of companies—auto manufacturers, furniture companies, publishing houses, ad agencies, design firms, flower shops—in several different industries. Many are self-employed.

Subjects to Study

Art, drawing, drafting, business, communication skills, English, computer skills

Discover More

On paper, redesign a room of your home. Check out magazines for ideas. Get paint and wallpaper samples from the hardware store. Will you re-cover the furniture in new fabric? Hang new drapes? Replace the flooring? Decide on a color scheme and draw the room.

Related Jobs

Visual artists, architects, landscape architects, engineers, photographers, and merchandise displayers

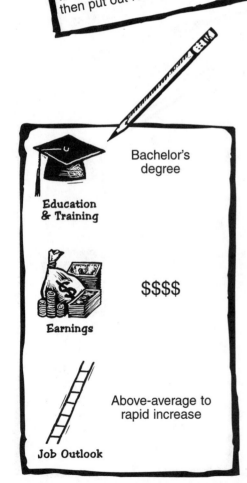

Education & Training
Bachelor's degree

Earnings
$$$$

Job Outlook
Above-average to rapid increase

Photographers & Camera Operators

On the Job

Photographers and camera operators use cameras, movie cameras, and camcorders to record people, places, and events on film. Most photographers specialize in commercial, portrait, or journalistic photography. They take school pictures, shoot portraits in a studio, or work for newspapers and magazines. Camera operators make documentaries, motion pictures, and industrial films. They may work long, irregular hours in places all over the world.

Something Extra

Photojournalists use their cameras to record history and news events for magazines and newspapers. It can be dangerous work. In some countries, journalists are easy targets for terrorists and the military. Reporting in war zones can be deadly, too. But photojournalists face these and other dangers to document the truth and give it to the world.

Subjects to Study

English, journalism, photography, art, creative writing, business, accounting

Discover More

Take photos of special people and places in your life. Try using different kinds of film and different lenses. For example, use black and white film to photograph your neighborhood. Use a telephoto lens to take pictures of small flowers and insects.

Related Jobs

Illustrators, designers, painters, sculptors, and editors

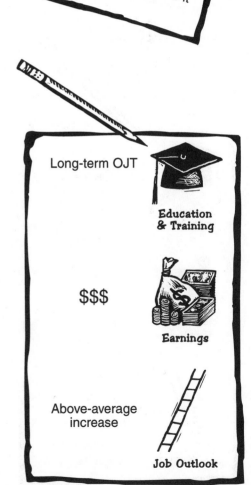

Long-term OJT

Education & Training

$$$

Earnings

Above-average increase

Job Outlook

Visual Artists

On the Job

Visual artists use a variety of methods and materials to communicate through art. They might use oil paints, watercolors, pencils, clay, chalk, or even scrap metal to create artworks. Visual artists are usually called graphic artists or fine artists.

Graphic artists use art to meet the needs of business clients, such as stores, ad agencies, and publishing firms. Fine artists create artwork to sell and display in museums or galleries. Many are self-employed.

Subjects to Study

Art, drawing, drafting, computer skills, English, communication skills, anatomy, business math

Discover More

The best way to prepare for this career is to take art classes, visit museums, study the styles of other artists, and practice, practice, practice.

Related Jobs

Account executives or creative directors, architects, display workers, designers, landscape architects, photographers, and art teachers

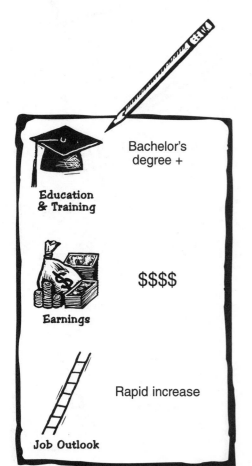

Education & Training
Bachelor's degree +

Earnings
$$$$

Job Outlook
Rapid increase

Actors, Directors, & Producers

On the Job

Actors, directors, and producers make words come alive through plays, TV shows, and films. Actors play characters, speaking the lines written in the script and adding their own movements. Directors choose plays and scripts, select the actors, and conduct rehearsals for productions. Producers arrange the financing and decide the size of the production and the budget. Directors and producers often work under tight deadlines and stressful conditions.

Something Extra

Making it as an actor is tough. That's why most actors work at least part-time at another job while they wait for their big break. For example, movie hunk Brad Pitt donned a chicken suit for a fast food restaurant. TV's Calista Flockhart worked as an aerobics instructor. And comedienne Whoopie Goldberg worked as a funeral parlor cosmetician, observing, "I'd rather work on dead people. They don't move."

Subjects to Study

English, public speaking, drama, music, dance, art, photography, communication skills

Discover More

You can learn more about the theater by auditioning for a role in a school or community play. If being on stage is not for you, try working backstage, making props, working the lights or sound system, or helping with costumes and makeup.

Related Jobs

Dancers, choreographers, drama teachers or coaches, radio and television announcers, stage managers, costume designers, makeup artists, lighting designers, and set designers

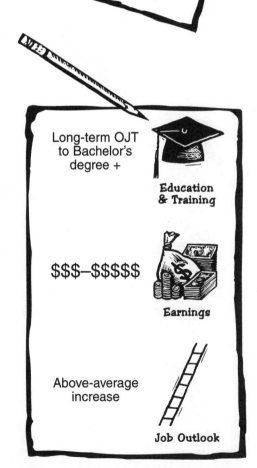

Long-term OJT to Bachelor's degree +

Education & Training

$$$–$$$$$

Earnings

Above-average increase

Job Outlook

Dancers & Choreographers

On the Job

Dancers express ideas and stories through the movement of their bodies. Dance styles include classical ballet, modern dance, tap, jazz, and different folk dances. Dancers perform in musicals, operas, TV shows, movies, music videos, and commercials. Dancers must be strong, coordinated, and dedicated. Choreographers create dances and teach dancers. They may work for one company or on a freelance basis. Most performances are in the evening and on weekends.

Subjects to Study

Music, dance, physical education, drama, English, history, literature

Discover More

Sign up for dance classes at a local studio. Try several styles, from ballet to tap to belly dancing. Ask the teacher about the job. Does he or she work at another job in addition to teaching? Does he or she perform with a company?

Related Jobs

Ice skaters, dance critics, dance instructors, recreational therapists, and athletes

Education & Training
Voc/tech training +

Earnings
$$$–$$$$

Job Outlook
Rapid increase

Musicians

On the Job

Musicians play instruments, sing, and write music for instrumental or vocal performances. They may perform in groups or alone, in front of live audiences, or in recording studios. They spend a lot of time rehearsing for performances. Most work nights and weekends and travel to perform. Because it is so hard to support themselves solely as musicians, many take other jobs as well. Many work in cities with recording studios, such as New York, Los Angeles, and Nashville.

Subjects to Study

Vocal music, instrumental music, English, creative writing, business math

Discover More

Participate in your school band, jazz band, or choir. Audition for a role in a school or community musical. Take lessons to learn a musical instrument.

Related Jobs

Booking agents, concert managers, music publishers, creative writers, and music store owners and managers

Something Extra

Did you ever wonder what famous musicians did before they were famous? Some, of course, hit it big early, but others had to work their way up from obscurity. Garth Brooks, for instance, beefed up as a nightclub bouncer, while Mariah Carey worked nights as a janitor in a beauty salon. As for Madonna, the ultimate material girl, she did counter duty at the Times Square Dunkin' Donuts.

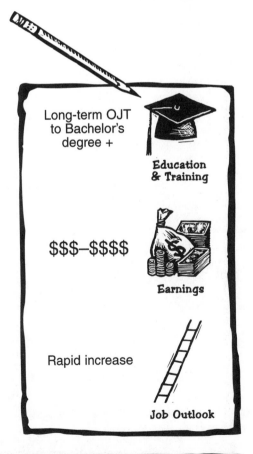

Long-term OJT to Bachelor's degree +

Education & Training

$$$–$$$$

Earnings

Rapid increase

Job Outlook

Marketing &
Sales Occupations

Cashiers

On the Job

Cashiers add up customers' bills, take their money, and give change. They also fill out charge forms for credit cards and give receipts. Cashiers are responsible for the money they collect during their shifts. They cannot leave their cash drawers without permission from their supervisor. Cashiers use cash registers, scanners, and computers regularly.

Subjects to Study

Math, English, communication skills, computer skills, typing, business

Discover More

Volunteer to work as a cashier at a church, club, or family rummage sale. Make sure you have enough money in the cash drawer to make change for the customers. Save the tags from the items paid for at your cash drawer. Add the total sales to the amount that was in your cash drawer before the sale. Then count the money in your drawer. Does it balance?

Related Jobs

Food counter clerks, bank tellers, counter and rental clerks, and sales clerks

Short-term OJT

Education & Training

$–$$

Earnings

Above-average increase

Job Outlook

Counter & Rental Clerks

On the Job

Counter and rental clerks take orders, figure out fees, receive payment, and accept returns. They answer questions about what kinds of items are in stock and how much they cost. They must know about the company's services and policies. Some fill out forms and tickets by hand, but most use computers and scanners.

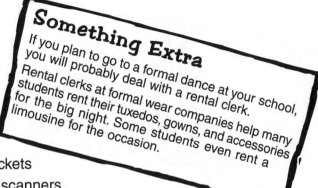

Something Extra

If you plan to go to a formal dance at your school, you will probably deal with a rental clerk. Rental clerks at formal wear companies help many students rent their tuxedos, gowns, and accessories for the big night. Some students even rent a limousine for the occasion.

Subjects to Study

Math, English, communication skills, computer skills, typing

Discover More

Go to a video store and rent a video. Watch what the rental clerk does to rent the item to you and to make sure that you will return it. Ask questions about the job.

Related Jobs

Cashiers, retail sales workers, food counter clerks, postal service clerks, and bank tellers

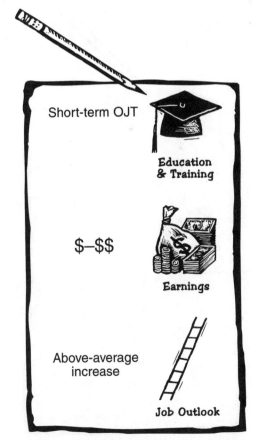

Short-term OJT

Education & Training

$–$$

Earnings

Above-average increase

Job Outlook

Insurance Agents & Brokers

Something Extra

People buy insurance to protect their assets. But not all assets are cars or houses. The famous insurance group Lloyd's of London has issued some odd insurance policies in recent years. Some of these policies include accident insurance for Russian cosmonauts traveling to the MIR space station; coverage in case of a crocodile attack; insuring a famous model's legs, a singer's vocal chords, and a food critic's taste buds.

On the Job

Insurance agents and brokers sell insurance policies to people and businesses. Insurance policies protect against different kinds of losses. Common policies include health, life, and car insurance. Insurance agents and brokers help people choose the policies that best meet their needs. Agents work for a single insurance company. Brokers are independent and sell insurance for several different companies. Agents and brokers often must schedule meetings in the evenings or on weekends.

Subjects to Study

Math, accounting, economics, government, psychology, sociology, speech, computer skills

Discover More

Ask your parents what kinds of insurance they have. How did they choose their insurance plans? Do they receive insurance through their employers?

Related Jobs

Real estate agents and brokers, securities and financial services sales representatives, financial advisors, estate planning specialists, and manufacturers' sales workers

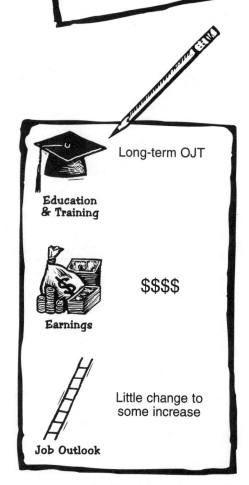

Long-term OJT

Education & Training

$$$$

Earnings

Little change to some increase

Job Outlook

Manufacturers' & Wholesale Sales Representatives

On the Job

Manufacturers' and wholesale sales representatives sell products to businesses, government agencies, and other institutions, often traveling for several days or weeks at a time. They answer questions about their products and show clients how the products can meet their needs and save them money. They also take orders and resolve problems or complaints about their merchandise.

Something Extra

Most sales representatives are paid on commission. Instead of receiving a regular paycheck, they get paid based on their sales: The more they sell, the more money they make. Few or no sales mean little or no money. High sales mean big paychecks. Salespeople must learn to budget and pay their bills knowing that their income is unpredictable.

Subjects to Study

Math, English, speech, communication skills, accounting, business, psychology, foreign languages, computer skills

Discover More

Think of some businesses in your community (such as hospitals, grocery stores, and restaurants) that might order products from manufacturers' sales representatives. What kind of products would each of these businesses buy?

Related Jobs

Retail service agents, real estate agents, insurance agents, securities sales workers, and wholesale and retail buyers

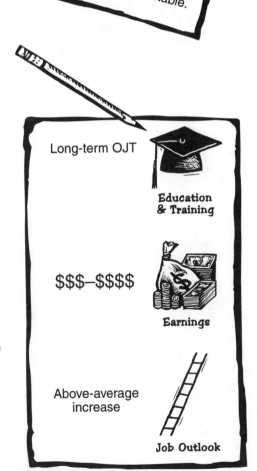

Long-term OJT

Education & Training

$$$–$$$$

Earnings

Above-average increase

Job Outlook

Real Estate Agents, Brokers, & Appraisers

Education & Training
Voc/tech training

Earnings
$$$$

Job Outlook
Average increase

On the Job

Real estate agents, brokers, and appraisers help people buy and sell homes and rental properties. Real estate agents show homes, help get financing, and make sure the contract conditions are met. Brokers may sell houses and rent and manage properties. Appraisers estimate the value of a property. All of these workers must know and understand their local housing market.

Subjects to Study

Math, English, accounting, economics, business, communication skills, computer skills, psychology

Discover More

You can usually find free real estate and rental magazines at grocery stores or drugstores. Look through one to find out what homes and properties are available in your community. How much do homes and apartments in your area cost?

Related Jobs

Automotive sales workers, securities and financial services sales workers, insurance agents and brokers, yacht brokers, travel agents, manufacturers' representatives, and art appraisers

Retail Sales Worker Supervisors & Managers

On the Job

Retail sales worker supervisors and managers work in all kinds of stores— dress shops, toy stores, convenience stores, and bakeries. They hire, train, and supervise workers. They also make the schedule of who will work what hours. They order supplies, keep the books, make bank deposits, and often wait on customers. Most work evenings and weekends.

Something Extra

Many people in our economy work "standard" workweek hours—8 A.M. to 5 P.M., Monday through Friday. They like having evenings and weekends free and knowing exactly when they will work. But other people thrive on different hours. Maybe you're a night person who enjoys working evenings. Or maybe you prefer working on a Saturday and taking a day off midweek, so you can hit the beach when it's not crowded. Retail managers often work nights and weekends but have time off midweek to do their own thing.

Subjects to Study

Math, English, psychology, business, communication skills, computer skills

Discover More

Visit a shop in your neighborhood and ask the manager if you can help out after school one or two days a week. You might help stock shelves or clean up. Watch the manager at work, and ask about the best and worst parts of the job.

Related Jobs

Managers in wholesale trade, hotels, banks, and hospitals

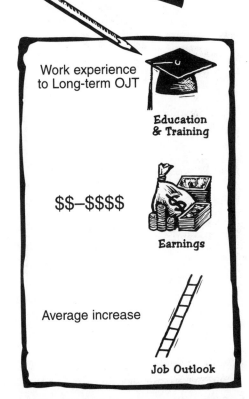

Work experience to Long-term OJT

Education & Training

$$–$$$$

Earnings

Average increase

Job Outlook

Retail Sales Workers

On the Job

Retail sales workers help customers choose and buy all kinds of items, from sweaters and makeup to lumber and plumbing. Their primary job is to interest customers in whatever products they are selling. They also fill out sales checks, take payment, bag purchases, and give change and receipts. Most sales workers are responsible for the money in their cash registers.

Subjects to Study

Math, English, communication skills, computer skills

Discover More

Watch the sales workers the next time you go shopping. What jobs do they do? How do they approach customers? How do they help you?

Related Jobs

Manufacturers' and wholesale trade sales workers, service sales representatives, counter and rental clerks, real estate sales agents, wholesale and retail buyers, insurance sales workers, and cashiers

Short-term OJT

Education & Training

$–$$$

Earnings

Average increase

Job Outlook

Securities & Financial Services Sales Representatives

On the Job

Securities sales representatives buy and sell stocks, bonds, and other financial products for clients who want to invest in the stock market. They explain terms and the advantages and disadvantages of different investments. Financial service sales representatives usually work for banks. They contact potential customers to sell their bank's services, which might include retirement planning and other investment services.

Subjects to Study

Math, English, communication skills, computer skills, speech, accounting, economics, psychology, government, business

Discover More

Find the stock market listings in the business section of your newspaper. Ask a parent or teacher to explain them to you. Listen to the stock market report on news programs or look up some stocks on the Internet.

Related Jobs

Insurance agents and real estate agents

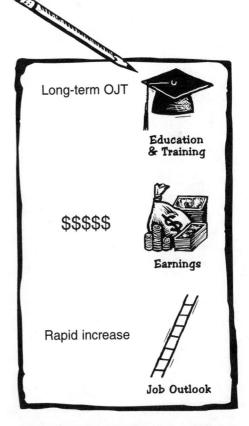

Long-term OJT

Education & Training

$$$$$

Earnings

Rapid increase

Job Outlook

Services Sales Representatives

On the Job

Services sales representatives work in many different fields. Some must travel to do their jobs, while others work from an office. A hotel sales representative contacts organizations to get their convention business. A telephone sales representative sells phone services for home or business use.

Services sales representatives often present their service as a way for the client to solve a problem.

Subjects to Study

Math, English, communication skills, computer skills, business, economics, psychology

Discover More

Participate in a fund-raising project for your school or another organization. Do you enjoy selling? Do sales workers win prizes? What did the winners do differently from others?

Related Jobs

Real estate agents, insurance agents, securities and financial services sales representatives, manufacturers' and wholesale sales representatives, and travel agents

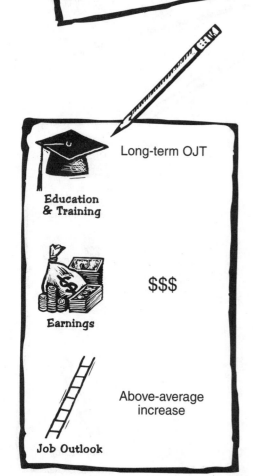

Long-term OJT

Education & Training

$$$

Earnings

Above-average increase

Job Outlook

Travel Agents

On the Job

Travel agents make hotel, airline, car rental, and cruise reservations for people and businesses. They plan group tours and conferences. They tell clients what papers they need to travel in foreign countries. They must be up to date on cultural and political issues, restaurants, and tourist attractions.

Something Extra

Where is Timbuktu? What country is also a continent? Where would you find Cape Canaveral? Do you ever play the game Trivial Pursuit®? Do you excel in the geography questions? If so, you might enjoy being a travel agent. These workers must have a good feel for geography, so they can help their clients plan their trips.

Subjects to Study

Communication skills, computer skills, typing, geography, English, foreign languages, history, math, business, accounting

Discover More

What foreign country are you curious about? Read about that country and find it on a map. Then find an Internet site where you can learn more about life in that country.

Related Jobs

Secretaries, tour guides, airline reservation agents, rental car agents; and travel counselors

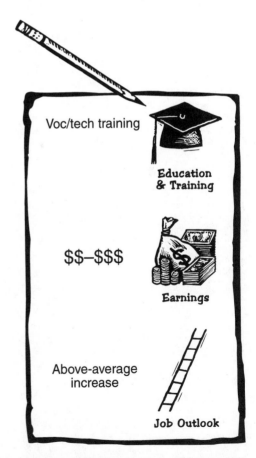

Voc/tech training

Education & Training

$$–$$$

Earnings

Above-average increase

Job Outlook

Administrative Support, Including Clerical Occupations

Adjusters, Investigators, & Collectors

On the Job

Insurance claims adjusters and claims investigators check to make sure that claims filed are covered by their company's policies. Then they decide how much should be paid and okay the payment. If the claim is not covered, they deny payment. Sometimes they travel to see damaged property, settle claims, or testify in court. Collectors notify customers of overdue, unpaid bills by letter and telephone and arrange for them to pay those bills.

Subjects to Study

Math, English, computer skills, economics, business, accounting, foreign languages, psychology, health

Discover More

Ask your parents if they have ever filed a claim on their car, home, life, or health insurance. Find out what they did to file the claim. Did they talk to an adjuster?

Related Jobs

Cost estimators, budget analysts, private investigators, auditing and reservation clerks, title searchers, human services workers, financial aid counselors, and probation officers

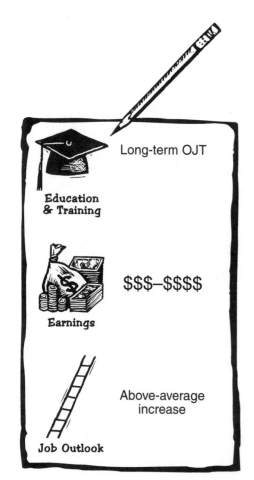

Education & Training
Long-term OJT

Earnings
$$$–$$$$

Job Outlook
Above-average increase

Bank Tellers

On the Job

Bank tellers cash checks, make deposits and withdrawals, and accept loan payments. They use computers to keep records. Tellers begin work before the bank opens by counting the cash in their drawers and end the workday by accurately balancing their cash drawers with the day's receipts. They must be friendly with customers, even when customers are rude to them.

Something Extra

Many people these days like to use their bank's automated teller machines (ATMs) to take out cash, make loan payments, and deposit money. ATMs are convenient because you can use them 24 hours a day, seven days a week. But with the convenience comes a risk: Many people have been robbed using their ATMs. Criminals find them convenient, too!

Subjects to Study

Math, English, communication skills, computer skills, typing, foreign languages, accounting, bookkeeping

Discover More

Open a savings or checking account at your local bank or credit union. Ask the teller to explain how to make deposits and withdrawals and how to use the ATM. Watch what the teller does as he or she helps you.

Related Jobs

New accounts clerks, cashiers, toll collectors, post office clerks, auction clerks, and ticket sellers

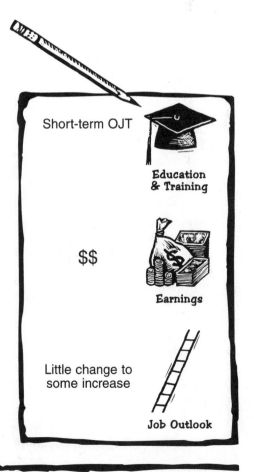

Short-term OJT

Education & Training

$$

Earnings

Little change to some increase

Job Outlook

Clerical Supervisors & Managers

On the Job

Clerical supervisors and managers make sure their employees work efficiently. If supplies are low or equipment needs to be repaired, they order new supplies or contract with a repair service. They train new employees, plan their work, and check their progress. They evaluate their employees' work habits, recommend pay raises and promotions, and sometimes must fire a worker.

Subjects to Study

English, communication skills, computer skills, business, math, speech, psychology

Discover More

Volunteer to manage a group project. Assign different parts of the project to different people and check their progress. You'll notice that everyone has his or her own way of doing things. What differences do you notice in the way each person works?

Related Jobs

Accounting clerks, cashiers, bank tellers, telephone operators, and managers

Short-term OJT +

Education & Training

$$$–$$$$

Earnings

Above-average increase

Job Outlook

Computer Operators

On the Job

Computer operators supervise computer hardware systems and keep them working smoothly. They watch for and try to prevent computer problems. On a daily basis, they might check the computer's controls and load tapes, paper, and disks as needed. When there is a computer error, they must locate and solve the problem.

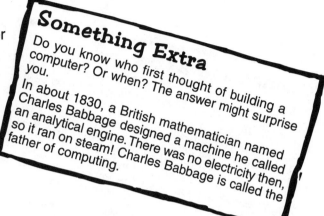

Something Extra

Do you know who first thought of building a computer? Or when? The answer might surprise you.

In about 1830, a British mathematician named Charles Babbage designed a machine he called an analytical engine. There was no electricity then, so it ran on steam! Charles Babbage is called the father of computing.

Subjects to Study

Math, English, communication skills, computer science, computer skills, typing

Discover More

How do blind people use computers? Visit your local library and ask if it has any talking or Braille computers. (Braille is a special kind of raised writing that blind people "read" with their finger-tips.) Sit in front of the computer, close your eyes, and try to use it.

Related Jobs

Computer scientists and systems analysts, programmers, computer service technicians, secretaries, typists, word processors, typesetters, and compositors

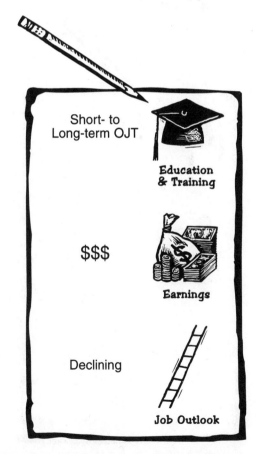

Short- to Long-term OJT

Education & Training

$$$

Earnings

Declining

Job Outlook

Court Reporters, Medical Transcriptionists, & Stenographers

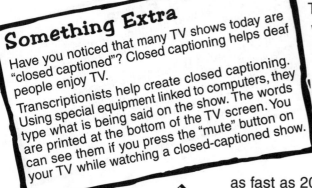

On the Job

These workers put spoken words into written form. Stenographers make notes using shorthand or a stenotype machine, which prints shorthand. Then they type up the notes so other people can read them. This is how court reporters record all statements made during court or government proceedings. Sometimes they type as fast as 200 words per minute. Because they are the only ones recording what is being said, they must be accurate.

Subjects to Study

English, stenographic skills, word processing, spelling, foreign languages, typing, computer skills, communication skills, listening skills

Discover More

Watch an actual court case on TV. Find the court reporter in the courtroom and watch what he or she does. Listen to all the statements made by the lawyers, witnesses, and judge. Try to imagine correctly recording every word they say.

Related Jobs

Bookkeepers, receptionists, secretaries, and administrative assistants

Education & Training
Voc/tech training

Earnings
$$$

Job Outlook
Little change to some increase

General Office Clerks

On the Job

General office clerks work in all kinds of businesses, from doctors' offices to banks, from big law firms to small companies. Because a business's needs change from day to day, so can a clerk's job duties. These workers file, type, keep records, prepare mailings, and proofread documents for mistakes. Senior clerks may be responsible for supervising other workers.

Something Extra

You don't need much experience to get an entry-level job as a general office clerk. These jobs are good ways to get your foot in the door of a company and gain experience. If you have good work habits and do your best, you can use an entry-level clerk job as a stepping stone to an even better job.

Subjects to Study

English, typing, word processing, computer skills, math, office practices, bookkeeping, accounting, business, spelling

Discover More

Can you type? Typing well is important in this and almost any other job. Many offices require clerks to type at least 60 words per minute. Take a typing class, practice, and become a good typist.

Related Jobs

Cashiers, teacher aides, and food and beverage workers

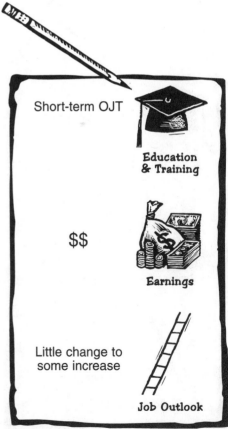

Short-term OJT

Education & Training

$$

Earnings

Little change to some increase

Job Outlook

Information Clerks

On the Job

Information clerks might be called hotel clerks, receptionists, airline reservation agents, or travel clerks. All information clerks either get information from people or answer questions about their employer's services or products. Their workdays are filled with answering multiline telephones, greeting visitors, helping customers, and using fax machines and computers.

Subjects to Study

English, communication skills, speech, computer skills, foreign languages, typing

Discover More

Do you know how your voice sounds on the telephone? Record a message in your normal speaking voice and play it back. If you don't like the way you sound, work on changing your voice and the way you speak.

Related Jobs

Dispatchers, security guards, bank tellers, guides, and telephone operators

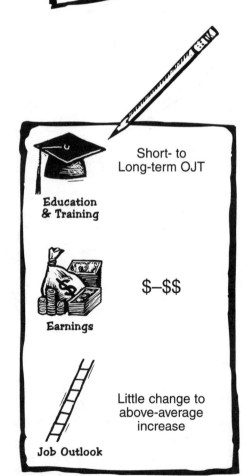

Education & Training
Short- to Long-term OJT

Earnings
$–$$

Job Outlook
Little change to above-average increase

Hotel & Motel Desk Clerks

On the Job

Hotel and motel desk clerks help guests check in and out of the inn, using computers to assign rooms. They answer questions about the local area and the establishment itself. They keep records of room assignments and collect payment from guests. In smaller motels, desk clerks may also act as bookkeepers and switchboard operators.

Something Extra

Someone once said, "If you want a real education in the ways of the world, work in a motel!" Hotel and motel desk clerks deal with all kinds of people from all over the world—many of whom are tired, lonely, or frustrated. Clerks must be friendly and courteous, even when a customer is yelling about lost reservations or bad service. They fix problems, answer questions, and soothe angry customers—and they must do it all with a smile.

Subjects to Study

Math, English, geography, psychology, communication skills, speech, typing, computer skills, foreign languages, bookkeeping

Discover More

If you were a desk clerk at a local hotel or motel, what places would you suggest that guests visit? Which restaurants would you recommend? Make a visitor's guide for your community.

Related Jobs

Dispatchers, security guards, bank tellers, guides, and telephone operators

Short- to Long-term OJT

Education & Training

$–$$

Earnings

Above-average increase

Job Outlook

Interviewing & New Accounts Clerks

On the Job

Interviewing clerks help people complete consumer surveys. New accounts clerks help people fill out bank account or charge card applications. They might work with people face to face, on the telephone, or by mail. Some interviewing clerks get financial and medical information before admitting patients to a hospital. Others verify information or create new files. Information clerks are sometimes called *customer service representatives*.

Subjects to Study

English, spelling, typing, communication skills, math, psychology, foreign languages

Discover More

Take a survey to find out what books your friends are reading. Ask for each book's title and author. Has the person read other books by that author? What kinds of books are your friends reading?

Related Jobs

Dispatchers, security guards, bank tellers, guides, and telephone operators

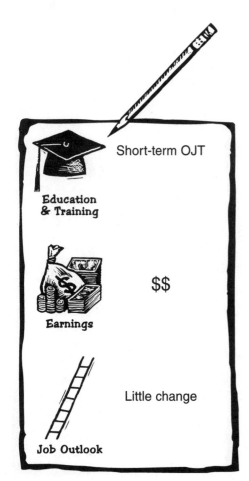

Education & Training — Short-term OJT

Earnings — $$

Job Outlook — Little change

Receptionists

On the Job

Receptionists greet customers on the phone and in person and refer them to the proper person or department. Making a good first impression is an important part of this job, since the receptionist is the first person most customers or clients meet. Receptionists use personal computers, fax machines, and multiline telephone systems to do their jobs.

Something Extra

Receptionists know who belongs where in an organization. Because of this, they are an important part of the security system at most companies. In larger companies, receptionists might give visitors identification cards or ask someone to escort a visitor to the proper office. They often are the first to meet visitors and the first to spot problems.

Subjects to Study

English, communication skills, spelling, speech, typing, computer skills, psychology, foreign languages, business

Discover More

Volunteer to be a greeter or an usher for a school play, a sports event, or a dance. Help people with their questions and concerns. Do you enjoy working with the public?

Related Jobs

Dispatchers, security guards, bank tellers, guides, and telephone operators

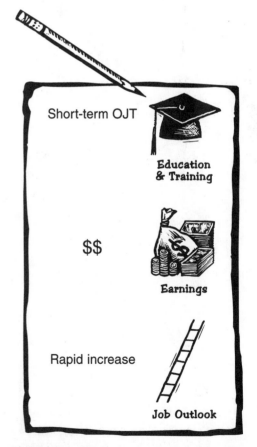

Short-term OJT

Education & Training

$$

Earnings

Rapid increase

Job Outlook

Reservation & Transportation Ticket Agents & Travel Clerks

On the Job

Reservation and transportation ticket agents make and confirm travel and hotel reservations, answer questions about rates and routes, and sell tickets. Travel clerks plan trips and offer travel suggestions. They tell their clients about tourist attractions, quality hotels, and good restaurants. These clerks and agents might work for travel clubs, airlines, hotels, or other businesses.

Subjects to Study

English, math, geography, communication skills, computer skills, foreign languages, psychology, typing, history

Discover More

Look through travel magazines or the travel section of a newspaper. Pick somewhere you would like to visit and send for information about it or look up sites on the Internet that have information about that place.

Related Jobs

Dispatchers, security guards, bank tellers, guides, and telephone operators

Education & Training

Short-term OJT

Earnings

$$$

Job Outlook

Little change to some decline

Loan Clerks & Credit Authorizers, Checkers, & Clerks

On the Job

Credit clerks collect and confirm information that people give when they apply for credit. Sometimes they investigate further by verifying employment or financial information. Credit authorizers research credit records and decide if customers have enough good credit to pay for what they want to buy.

Something Extra

Anyone who has a credit card or who has taken out a loan to buy something has a credit history. Credit bureaus keep track of these histories. You will start creating your credit history the first time you buy something on credit. If you don't pay your bills on time, your credit report will show that. If you make a habit of not paying your bills on time, you might not be able to buy a house or a car that you want.

Subjects to Study

English, communication skills, computer skills, math, typing

Discover More

Ask your parents if they know what information is in their credit histories. What credit cards do they have? Ask them if they have a house or car loan. How much do they owe on their loans?

Related Jobs

Claim examiners and adjusters, customer-complaint clerks, procurement clerks, probate clerks, and collection clerks

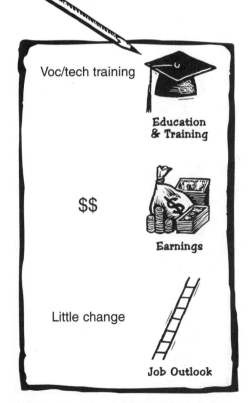

Voc/tech training

Education & Training

$$

Earnings

Little change

Job Outlook

Mail Clerks & Messengers

On the Job

Mail clerks usually work in large companies, where they sort and deliver mail to other employees. They also prepare the mail that is sent outside the company. Messengers drive, walk, or ride bicycles to pick up and deliver letters and packages that must be delivered quickly. Many work for courier services. Some messengers are paid by how many deliveries they make and how far they travel.

Subjects to Study

Computer skills, communication skills, listening skills, driver education, geography, English, math, physical education, typing

Discover More

Only e-mail and fax machines can deliver copies across town faster than a messenger. But sometimes an original copy is needed. Choose a document and send it to someone by fax machine and e-mail. Look at the faxed and e-mailed copies of the document. How are they different from your original?

Related Jobs

Postal clerks, mail carriers, route drivers, and traffic, shipping, and receiving clerks

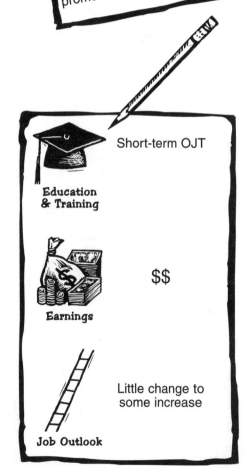

Education & Training — Short-term OJT

Earnings — $$

Job Outlook — Little change to some increase

Material Recording, Scheduling, Dispatching, & Distributing Workers

On the Job

Material recording, scheduling, dispatching, and distributing workers coordinate and keep track of orders for personnel, equipment, and materials. Clerks unpack, verify, and record arriving merchandise. Dispatchers working for utility companies or fire and police departments send crews where they are needed.

Something Extra

Materials and distribution workers are the people who make sure you get the products you order. For example, if a warehouse worker makes a mistake in recording what materials a company has in stock, you might be told that what you want is out of stock, even if it is there. If the distribution workers don't do their job, you could receive something you didn't order.

Subjects to Study

Math, computer skills, typing, communication skills, speech, English, physical education, psychology

Discover More

You need to be organized to keep track of materials. Make an inventory of the materials you use at school. What items do you need to restock?

Related Jobs

Airline radio operators, airline dispatchers, air traffic controllers, stock clerks, material clerks, distributing clerks, and routing clerks

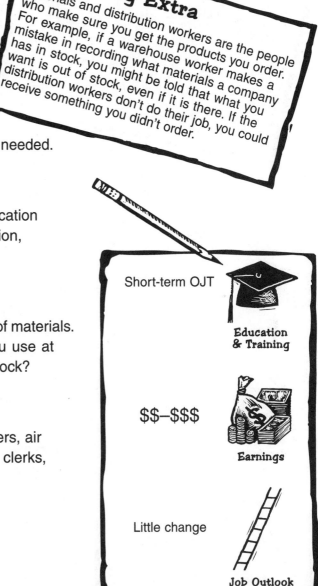

Short-term OJT

Education & Training

$$–$$$

Earnings

Little change

Job Outlook

Dispatchers

On the Job

Dispatchers receive emergency calls, find out where help is needed and how serious the situation is, and send police, firefighters, or ambulances to the scene. Dispatchers in transportation coordinate arrivals and departures of shipments to meet specific time schedules. All dispatchers keep records of the calls they receive and what they do about them.

Subjects to Study

English, computer skills, typing, communication skills, psychology, foreign languages

Discover More

Learn how to contact emergency help in your community. Visit a fire or police station and ask for permission to watch a dispatcher work.

Related Jobs

Airline radio operators, airline dispatchers, air traffic controllers, telephone operators, customer service representatives, and transportation agents

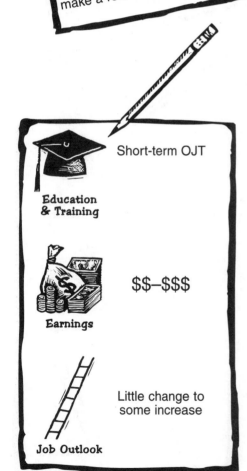

Education & Training — Short-term OJT

Earnings — $$–$$$

Job Outlook — Little change to some increase

Stock Clerks

On the Job

Stock clerks receive, unpack, and check materials into the stockroom. They keep records of items entering and leaving the stockroom and report damaged or spoiled products. They bring items to the sales floor and stock shelves. Many stock clerks work for department or grocery stores.

Something Extra

An inventory is made up of all the products a business has on hand. A business must know what products it has if it is going to be successful. Bar code systems are the most popular way to track inventory. Bar codes are the black stripes you see on items you buy. Stock clerks use hand-held scanners to read bar codes. This helps keep the inventory accurate. A bar code appears on the back of this book.

Subjects to Study

English, math, computer skills, physical education, bookkeeping

Discover More

Visit a grocery or warehouse-style store. Are there any stock clerks working on the floor? If so, notice how they organize products on the shelves. Ask what they like about the job.

Related Jobs

Shipping and receiving clerks, distributing clerks, routing clerks, stock supervisors, and cargo checkers

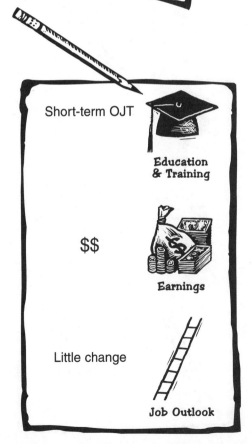

Short-term OJT

Education & Training

$$

Earnings

Little change

Job Outlook

Traffic, Shipping, & Receiving Clerks

On the Job

Traffic clerks keep records of all freight coming in and leaving a company and make sure the company is charged correctly. Shipping clerks keep records on all outgoing shipments. They fill orders from the stockroom and direct workers who load products onto trucks. Receiving clerks check materials coming into the warehouse, make sure they are in good condition, and send them to the right departments.

Subjects to Study

Math, computer skills, business, bookkeeping, typing

Discover More

Make a list of basic items you use every day, such as toothpaste, tissues, soap, and shampoo. Check your personal inventory. What items do you need to restock?

Related Jobs

Stock clerks, material clerks, distributing clerks, routing clerks, express clerks, expediters, and order fillers

Education & Training — Short-term OJT

Earnings — $$

Job Outlook — Little change to some increase

Postal Clerks & Mail Carriers

On the Job

Postal clerks sort mail for delivery, sell stamps, weigh packages, and help customers file claims for damaged packages. Mail carriers deliver the mail to homes and businesses on foot or by car. They also pick up mail from homes and businesses on their route.

Something Extra

Optical character readers (OCRs) and bar code sorters make sorting mail much easier and faster than it used to be. They also make it less likely that mail will go to the wrong address. How do they work?

OCRs "read" the address line and the ZIP code at a speed of nine letters per second. The bar code is "sprayed" onto the mail, which is then sorted by as many as three different computers.

Subjects to Study

English, physical education, driver education, communication skills, computer skills

Discover More

Find out who delivers your mail and talk to your carrier about his or her job. Does your carrier walk or drive? What are the working hours? What does your carrier like or dislike about the job?

Related Jobs

Mail clerks, file clerks, routing clerks, sorters, material moving equipment operators, clerk typists, cashiers, data entry operators, messengers, and delivery truck drivers

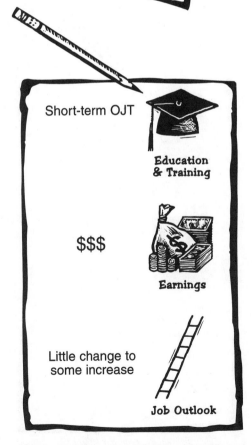

Short-term OJT

Education & Training

$$$

Earnings

Little change to some increase

Job Outlook

Record Clerks

On the Job

Record clerks take care of all kinds of business records, including billing information, customer orders, and employee files. In a small business, one clerk may handle all of these records. Large businesses often hire several different clerks to take care of different types of files.

Subjects to Study

Business math, computer skills, office skills, typing, accounting, bookkeeping, English, spelling

Discover More

Talk with your parents about their financial records. How do they keep track of bills that are due? How do they know what bills they have already paid? Who is the record clerk in your family?

Related Jobs

Bank tellers, receiving clerks, health information clerks, hotel and motel desk clerks, credit clerks, and reservation and transportation ticket agents

Short-term OJT

Education & Training

$$

Earnings

Little change to some increase

Job Outlook

Billing Clerks & Billing Machine Operators

On the Job

Billing clerks keep records of customers' charges and payments. They calculate the total amount due from a customer and prepare a detailed bill showing any new charges and payments. Billing machine operators print out bills and invoices, which are sent to customers.

Something Extra

Companies used to print customer bills using special billing machines. These machines were like computers, but could not do anything except prepare bills.

Today, computers have replaced most billing machines. Using computers, a clerk can compute charges and prepare bills in just one step, saving a lot of time.

Subjects to Study

Math, computer skills, office skills, English, typing, accounting, bookkeeping, business

Discover More

Ask your parents to show you some of the bills they receive. What information is included on each bill? Ask what the terms "transaction date" and "closing date" mean.

Related Jobs

Bank tellers, receiving clerks, health information clerks, hotel and motel clerks, credit clerks, and reservation and transportation ticket agents

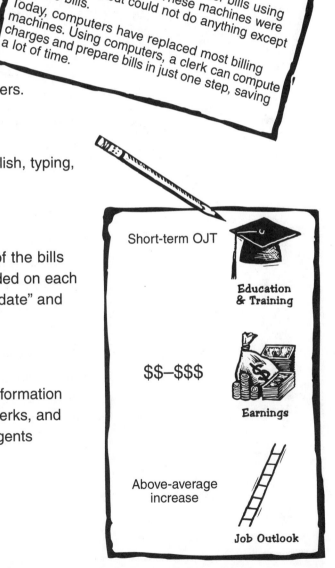

Short-term OJT

Education & Training

$$–$$$

Earnings

Above-average increase

Job Outlook

Bookkeeping, Accounting, & Auditing Clerks

On the Job

Bookkeeping and accounting clerks keep records of all the money spent and received by their company. They prepare reports, post bank deposits, and pay bills. Auditing clerks check the financial records of other employees in an organization and correct any errors they find.

Subjects to Study

Math, office skills, computer skills, English, business, accounting

Discover More

Keep your own financial records. Use a notebook to record any money you receive from allowance, gifts, or chores. Then record how you spend your money. Keep your receipts and banking records in a file.

Related Jobs

Bank tellers, statistical clerks, receiving clerks, medical record clerks, hotel and motel clerks, credit clerks, and reservation and transportation ticket agents

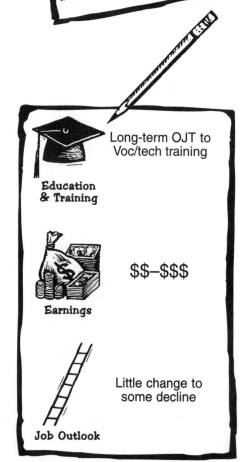

Long-term OJT to Voc/tech training

Education & Training

$$–$$$

Earnings

Little change to some decline

Job Outlook

Brokerage Clerks & Statement Clerks

On the Job

Brokerage clerks record the sale and purchase of stocks, bonds, and other investments. Statement clerks use high-speed machines that help them provide bank customers with account statements each month. These machines fold the statement and place it in an envelope, which is then mailed to the bank customer.

Something Extra

It used to be that if you wrote a check, you got the canceled check back from your bank. You could use the canceled check if you had to prove payment. But many banks today do not return canceled checks to their customers. They send only the account statement and keep copies of the checks on file. This reduces their labor and mailing costs, but it may raise yours. If you must prove payment, you have to order your canceled checks from the bank—and pay for them.

Subjects to Study

Math, office skills, computer skills, English

Discover More

Ask your parents to show you their checking account monthly statement. Notice the information by the bank that is given to the customer. Did your parents receive canceled checks with their statement?

Related Jobs

Bank tellers, receiving clerks, medical record clerks, hotel and motel clerks, credit clerks, and reservation and transportation clerks

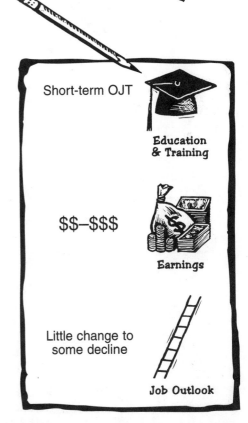

Short-term OJT

Education & Training

$$–$$$

Earnings

Little change to some decline

Job Outlook

File Clerks

On the Job

File clerks sort, store, retrieve, and update office records filed according to a company's system. They examine incoming information and mark it with a number or letter code. They store the information in a paper file or enter the information into a computer file. When someone in the company needs information from a file, the clerk retrieves it.

Subjects to Study

English, office skills, typing, computer skills

Discover More

Set up a filing system at home, using a file cabinet, folders, or a simple cardboard box. Keep your report cards, medical records, information about sports and activities, and your financial records in it.

Related Jobs

Bank tellers, receiving clerks, health information clerks, hotel and motel clerks, credit clerks, and reservation and transportation clerks

Education & Training
Short-term OJT

Earnings
$$

Job Outlook
Little change to some increase

Library Assistants & Bookmobile Drivers

On the Job

Library assistants lend and collect books, issue library cards, and repair books. They provide special help to people who can't see well. Bookmobile drivers drive vans or trucks stocked with books to different places, such as hospitals, nursing homes, and schools. They lend and collect books, collect fines, and act as links between the library and the community.

Something Extra

Andrew Carnegie was a poor man when he came to the United States from Scotland. In America, however, he made millions of dollars in the steel industry. When he sold his interest in the industry, he gave most of his fortune away to charity. Today, many cities across the country owe their free public libraries to the money Mr. Carnegie donated.

Subjects to Study

English, business math, computer skills, office skills, driver education

Discover More

Visit a bookmobile in your community and talk to the driver about this job. Notice the people visiting the bookmobile and the types of books they check out. How does the driver keep track of the transactions?

Related Jobs

Bank tellers, receiving clerks, health information clerks, hotel and motel clerks, credit clerks, and reservation and transportation ticket agents

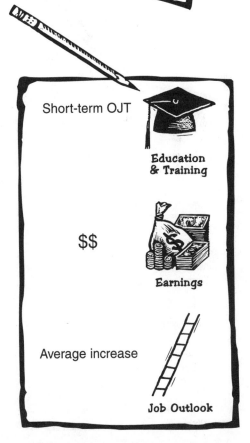

Short-term OJT

Education & Training

$$

Earnings

Average increase

Job Outlook

Order Clerks

On the Job

Order clerks receive and fill requests for machine parts, movie rentals, clothing, foods, and all kinds of other items. After completing the order, they send it to the proper department to be filled. They may fill orders from other employees inside a business, from salespeople, or from customers. Most work regular workday hours, but some must work nights and weekends.

Subjects to Study

Math, English, foreign languages, computer skills, office skills

Discover More

Look through a catalog and read the directions for placing an order. Fill out the order form for the products you'd like to buy. Make sure you give all the information asked for on the form. Figure out what your order would cost, including tax and shipping charges.

Related Jobs

Bank tellers, receiving clerks, health information clerks, hotel and motel clerks, credit clerks, and reservation and transportation ticket agents

Education & Training
Short-term OJT

Earnings
$$

Job Outlook
Little change

Payroll & Time-Keeping Clerks

On the Job

Payroll and time-keeping clerks make sure that workers get their paychecks on time and that the checks are for the right amount. Time-keeping clerks collect timecards from employees and check them for errors. Payroll clerks figure a worker's pay by adding up the hours worked and subtracting taxes, insurance, and other deductions.

Something Extra

Have you heard the term *fringe benefits*? These are a kind of extra payment from your employer. Fringe benefits might include paid vacations and holidays, sick days, health insurance, tuition assistance, and employee discounts. Sometimes, a job's fringe benefits can make a lower-paying job an attractive one. For example, some people like working in movie theaters because they can see all the latest movies for free.

Subjects to Study

Math, office skills, computer skills, English

Discover More

Ask your parents to show you their paycheck stubs. Notice the difference between the "gross" and "net" earnings. Find out what costs (such as insurance, taxes, and savings plans) are deducted from the paycheck. These are called "deductions."

Related Jobs

Bank tellers, receiving clerks, health information clerks, hotel and motel clerks, credit clerks, and reservation and transportation ticket agents

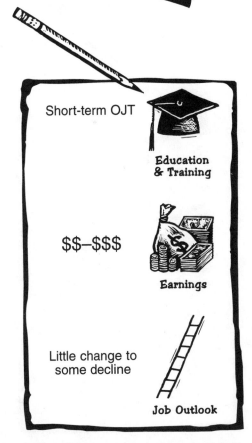

Short-term OJT

Education & Training

$$–$$$

Earnings

Little change to some decline

Job Outlook

Personnel Clerks

On the Job

Personnel clerks work with people who are applying for jobs in their company as well as with newly hired workers. They explain company rules, dress codes, pay policies, and benefits. They also maintain employee records and notify employees of job openings in the company.

Subjects to Study

English, speech, communication skills, office skills, computer skills

Discover More

Get a job application from a business and look at the kind of information it asks for. Practice filling one out. If you can't get an application from a business, check the library for books with examples of job applications.

Related Jobs

Bank tellers, receiving clerks, health information clerks, hotel and motel clerks, credit clerks, and reservation and transportation ticket agents

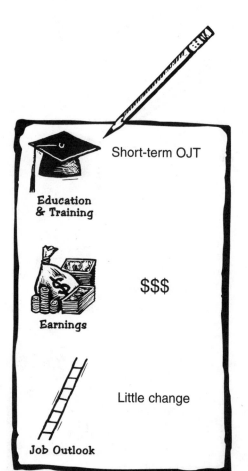

Short-term OJT

Education & Training

$$$

Earnings

Little change

Job Outlook

Secretaries

On the Job

Secretaries help keep offices organized and running smoothly. They schedule appointments, maintain files, type correspondence, greet visitors, and answer telephone calls. They work with office equipment such as computers, fax machines, and copiers. They may supervise clerks and other office workers. Some, such as medical and legal secretaries, do highly specialized work.

Something Extra

In days past, people thought of secretaries as low-level gophers, young women who typed, answered phones, and made coffee. Today's reality is much different. A secretary today is a kind of junior executive, the keeper of the office schedules and key information, the gatekeeper to the boss's door. Men and women working as secretaries often have access to confidential information and the company credit card. Most business people know that a company is only as good as its secretaries!

Subjects to Study

English, spelling, grammar, speech, typing, computer skills, office skills, math

Discover More

Talk to the secretaries at your school about their training and job duties. Develop some office skills, such as typing, filing, and word processing.

Related Jobs

Bookkeepers, receptionists, stenographers, personnel clerks, typists, word processors, legal assistants, medical assistants, office managers, and human resource workers

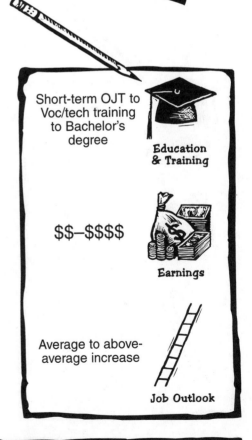

Short-term OJT to Voc/tech training to Bachelor's degree

Education & Training

$$–$$$$

Earnings

Average to above-average increase

Job Outlook

Teacher Aides

On the Job

Teacher aides help children in the classroom and school cafeteria or on the playground and field trips. Sometimes they pay special attention to individual students or small groups who need more help with a subject. They help teachers by grading papers, keeping attendance records, typing, filing, ordering supplies, helping out in the computer lab, or preparing class lessons.

Subjects to Study

English, communication skills, office skills, computer skills, math, foreign languages, speech

Discover More

Volunteer to help care for younger children at your school, church, or a local daycare center or youth organization. You might help them with schoolwork, play games, or teach a craft.

Related Jobs

Preschool teachers and child-care workers, family daycare providers, library technicians, and library assistants

Short-term OJT

Education & Training

$$

Earnings

Rapid increase

Job Outlook

Telephone Operators

On the Job

Telephone operators help customers when calls cannot be dialed directly, such as person-to-person or collect calls. They give customers refunds when calls are not made properly. They help handle emergency calls and give out local and long-distance telephone numbers.

Something Extra

Hablá Español? If you want to be an international telephone operator, you'd better speak a second language. People placing international calls don't always know the language of the person answering the phone. So the operator acts as the link, helping make sure the call reaches the person it's supposed to.

Subjects to Study

English, business math, computer skills, speech, foreign languages, office skills, listening skills, typing

Discover More

Do you have good listening skills? Do you take accurate notes in class? Show your notes to your teachers and ask if they are accurate. Ask a teacher to explain the difference between active and passive listening.

Related Jobs

Customer service representatives, dispatchers, hotel clerks, information clerks, police aides, receptionists, reservation agents, and travel clerks

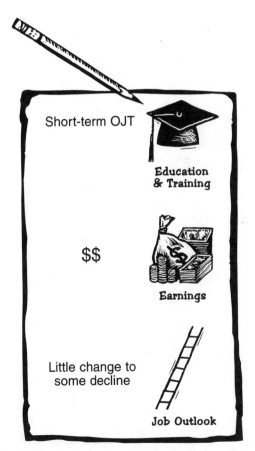

Short-term OJT

Education & Training

$$

Earnings

Little change to some decline

Job Outlook

Typists, Word Processors, & Data Entry Keyers

On the Job

Typists and word processors set up and type reports, letters, manuscripts and mailing labels. They may have other office duties as well, such as filing, answering telephones, and sorting mail. Data entry keyers fill out forms that appear on computer screens or enter lists of items or numbers. Sometimes they also proofread and edit documents.

Subjects to Study

English, office skills, computer skills, typing, spelling, punctuation, grammar

Discover More

Before you begin a career in this field, you must type at least 50 words per minute accurately. Practice typing so that you become a faster and better typist. The more you practice, the easier it becomes!

Related Jobs

Secretaries, stenographers, court reporters, dispatchers, and telephone operators

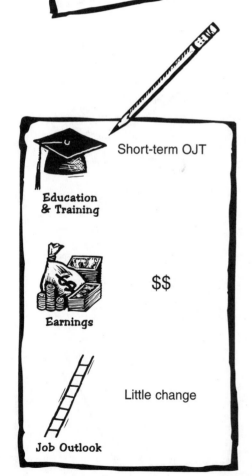

Short-term OJT

Education & Training

$$

Earnings

Little change

Job Outlook

Service
Occupations

Chefs, Cooks, & Other Kitchen Workers

On the Job

Chefs and cooks plan and make meals in restaurants, schools, cafeterias, and hospitals. They supervise other workers, order supplies, and plan menus. Kitchen workers help chefs and cooks by chopping vegetables, measuring ingredients, and stirring soups and sauces. They also keep the kitchen clean and wash dishes. These workers are on their feet all day in crowded, hot kitchens. Most work evenings and weekends, and many work part-time.

Subjects to Study

Home economics, nutrition, vocational education, math, health

Discover More

Plan your family's dinner menus for a week. Make a grocery list for your meals, then go with a parent to the store and get your ingredients. Help out in the kitchen to make your meals.

Related Jobs

Butchers and meat cutters, cannery workers, and industrial bakers

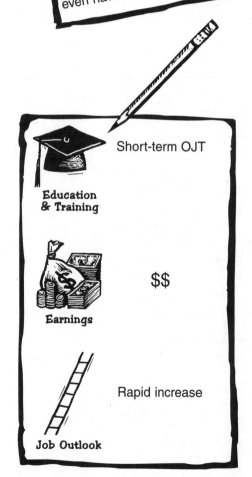

Short-term OJT

Education & Training

$$

Earnings

Rapid increase

Job Outlook

Food & Beverage Service Workers

On the Job

Food and beverage service workers deal with customers in restaurants. They take food orders, fill drink orders, serve food, prepare the bill, and may accept payment. Other workers clean dirty tables and reset them with silverware and napkins. These workers spend hours on their feet. They carry heavy trays and must serve customers quickly and courteously. Most work evenings and weekends, and many work part-time.

Subjects to Study

English, foreign languages, math, accounting, speech

Discover More

The best way to learn about the restaurant industry is to work in it. Look for a part-time job at a fast-food restaurant. Or talk to friends who have worked in one. Find out what they liked and disliked about the job. What hours and days did they work?

Related Jobs

Flight attendants, butlers, and tour bus drivers

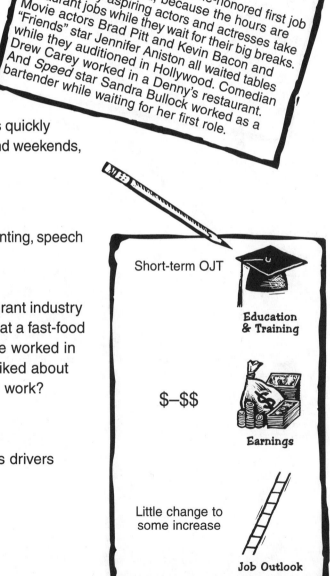

Short-term OJT

Education & Training

$–$$

Earnings

Little change to some increase

Job Outlook

Dental Assistants

On the Job

Dental assistants help dentists during patient exams and treatments. They schedule appointments, keep patient records, handle billing, and order supplies. Those with lab duties clean removable dentures and make temporary crowns for teeth. They wear gloves and masks to protect themselves from diseases and germs. Many work evenings and Saturdays, and they spend a good part of their time on their feet.

Subjects to Study

Biology, chemistry, health, business, math, computer skills, psychology

Discover More

Visit your dentist's office and ask about careers in this field. Does your dentist employ an assistant? What does he or she do? Ask the assistant about training and the job.

Related Jobs

Medical assistants, physical therapy assistants, occupational therapy assistants, pharmacy assistants, and veterinary technicians

Education & Training
Long-term OJT to Voc/tech training

Earnings
$$–$$$

Job Outlook
Rapid increase

Medical Assistants

On the Job

Medical assistants help keep your doctor's office running smoothly. They answer phones, greet patients, schedule appointments, arrange for hospital admissions and tests, handle billing, and file records. They may take medical histories, explain treatments to patients, and help doctors with exams. They must have good people skills. Many work evenings and weekends.

Subjects to Study

Math, health, biology, typing, bookkeeping, computer skills, office skills, English, foreign languages

Discover More

Ask your own doctor if you can spend a day in the office, watching what the medical assistants do. Maybe you can help file papers, answer phones, or make copies.

Related Jobs

Medical secretaries, hospital clerks, pharmacy helpers, health information technicians, dental assistants, and occupational and physical therapy aides

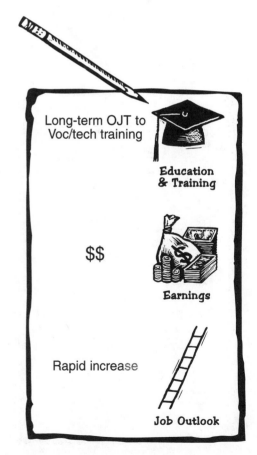

Long-term OJT to Voc/tech training

Education & Training

$$

Earnings

Rapid increase

Job Outlook

Nursing Aides & Psychiatric Aides

On the Job

Nursing and psychiatric aides care for patients in hospitals, nursing homes, and mental health clinics. They feed, bathe, and dress patients, help them get in and out of bed, take temperatures and blood pressures, and set up equipment. They report any signs or changes that might be important for the doctors or nurses to know. Most work some weekends and evening hours. They must be strong enough to lift and move patients.

Subjects to Study

Health, nutrition, anatomy, communication skills, English, psychology

Discover More

Volunteer at a nursing home in your community. You might be asked to read to patients, make deliveries, help with activities, or just visit with a patient who is lonely.

Related Jobs

Homemaker-home health aides, child-care attendants, companions, and occupational and physical therapy aides

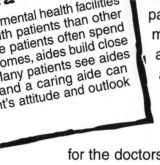

Education & Training — Short-term OJT

Earnings — $$

Job Outlook — Rapid increase

Occupational Therapy Assistants & Aides

On the Job

Occupational therapy assistants help therapists in clinics, rehab centers, nursing homes, and home health care programs. They help injured patients regain use of damaged muscles. They might also help patients learn to use wheelchairs or other devices. They also help mentally disabled patients learn living skills like cooking and keeping a checkbook. Occupational therapy aides keep patient records and set up equipment. These workers must be strong enough to lift and move patients and equipment.

Something Extra

Some people enjoy the 9-to-5 routine. But for many others, spending eight hours a day behind a desk would be torture. Occupational therapy assistants who work with mentally disabled adults may travel to several homes and facilities each day, taking clients grocery shopping, teaching them cooking skills, helping them apply for assistance, or driving them on errands.

Subjects to Study

Health, anatomy, physical education, communication skills, English, psychology

Discover More

Try teaching younger children an activity or game. Plan out the activity, decide whether it's appropriate for their age group, then teach the children how to play. Watch to make sure they play fairly and safely.

Related Jobs

Physical therapy assistants and aides, dental assistants, medical assistants, and pharmacy assistants

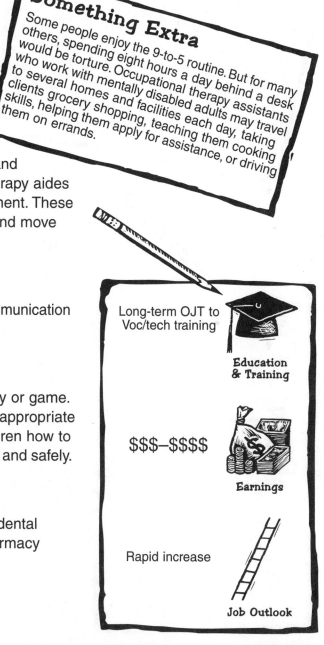

Long-term OJT to Voc/tech training

Education & Training

$$$–$$$$

Earnings

Rapid increase

Job Outlook

Physical & Corrective Therapy Assistants & Aides

On the Job

Physical therapy assistants help physical therapists care for patients in hospitals, nursing homes, and home health care programs. They help patients recovering from injuries or disease improve their mobility, relieve pain, and regain muscle use. They may help with exercises, give massages, and apply hot/cold packs. Physical therapy aides keep equipment in good order, move patients to and from the treatment area, and help with record keeping.

Subjects to Study

Health, anatomy, physical education, communication skills, English, psychology

Discover More

Ask your gym teacher to show you some exercises you can use to strengthen your own muscles. Then teach these exercises to family members or friends. Set up a regular exercise schedule for yourself.

Related Jobs

Dental assistants, medical assistants, occupational therapy assistants and aides, and recreational therapy assistants

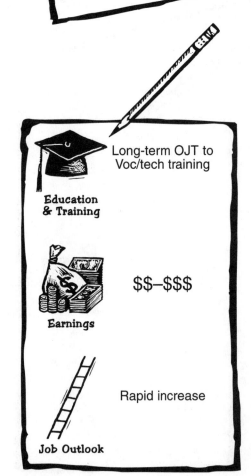

Education & Training
Long-term OJT to Voc/tech training

Earnings
$$–$$$

Job Outlook
Rapid increase

Barbers & Cosmetologists

On the Job

Barbers and cosmetologists help people look their best. They cut, shampoo, style, color, and perm hair. They may fit customers for hairpieces, shave male customers, and give facial massages and advice on makeup. Many cosmetologists are trained to give manicures. They also keep customer records and order supplies. These workers spend a lot of time on their feet. Many work part time, and many are self-employed.

Subjects to Study

Communication skills, business, accounting, speech, health

Discover More

Set up a beauty salon at home and practice on yourself or a friend. Look through magazines for the latest styles, then wash and style your friend's hair, and give him or her a facial.

Related Jobs

Instructors, beauty supply distributors, manicurists, and makeup artists

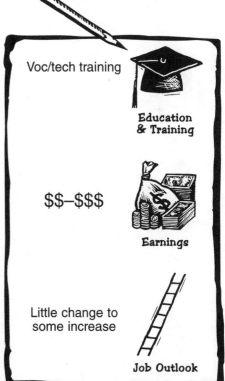

Voc/tech training

Education & Training

$$–$$$

Earnings

Little change to some increase

Job Outlook

Flight Attendants

On the Job

Flight attendants help keep airline passengers safe and comfortable. In an emergency, they help passengers react calmly and quickly. They also stock the plane with food, drinks, blankets, first aid kits, and other supplies. During the flight, they serve food and drinks and answer questions. They may administer first aid to passengers who become ill. They work long, irregular hours, travel extensively, and spend hours on their feet. They must remain calm in emergencies.

Subjects to Study

English, communication skills, foreign languages, speech, first aid, health, physical education

Discover More

For more information on becoming a flight attendant, write to the Association of Flight Attendants, 1625 Massachusetts Ave. NW, 3rd Floor, Washington, DC 20036.

Related Jobs

Emergency medical technicians, firefighters, maritime crews, and camp counselors

Education & Training
Long-term OJT to Voc/tech training

Earnings
$$$$

Job Outlook
Rapid increase

Homemaker-Home Health Aides

On the Job

Homemaker-home health aides help elderly, disabled, and seriously ill patients to live at home instead of in a nursing home. They clean, do laundry, prepare meals, and help with personal hygiene. They also check the patient's pulse and blood pressure and give medication. Aides keep records of each patient's condition and progress. They often work part-time and weekend hours.

Something Extra

When is a pet not a pet? When it's a trained companion for a disabled person. Today, many people who are wheelchair-bound have trained monkeys who help them live independently. These little animals perform simple household tasks, fetch items for their owners, dial the phone, even call for help in an emergency. Although their conversation skills are limited, trained animals allow their owners to live at home and provide companionship and love.

Subjects to Study

Home economics, nutrition, health, first aid, English, foreign languages

Discover More

Set up your own "rent-a-kid" service in your neighborhood. Can you help out in your neighbors' homes by cleaning, ironing clothes, running errands, or doing yard work to earn extra money?

Related Jobs

Child-care attendants in schools, companions, nursing and psychiatric aides, preschool workers, occupational therapy aides, and physical therapy aides

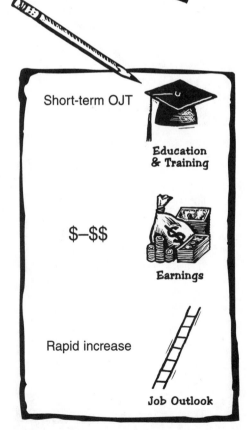

Short-term OJT

Education & Training

$–$$

Earnings

Rapid increase

Job Outlook

Janitors, Cleaners, & Cleaning Supervisors

On the Job

Janitors, cleaners, and cleaning supervisors keep offices, schools, hospitals, hotels, and other public buildings clean and in good condition. They clean, repair, empty trash cans, paint, and mow lawns. Cleaning supervisors assign jobs, supervise workers, and order supplies. These workers often work evenings and weekends. The work can be dirty and strenuous.

Subjects to Study

Shop courses, home economics, physical education, accounting

Discover More

Talk to the janitor at your school. Make a list of all the chores and different tasks he or she does. Ask about the best part of the job. What is the worst part of the job?

Related Jobs

Refuse collectors, floor waxers, street sweepers, window cleaners, gardeners, boiler tenders, pest controllers, and general maintenance repairers

Education & Training
Short-term OJT +

Earnings
$$–$$$$

Job Outlook
Little change to some increase

Landscaping, Grounds-Keeping, Nursery, Greenhouse, & Lawn Service Workers

On the Job

These workers care for lawns, trees, gardens, and other plants and keep the grounds free of litter. They may prune, feed, and water gardens and mow and water lawns at private homes and public places. They also maintain athletic fields, golf courses, cemeteries, and parks. They work outside in all kinds of weather. Many are self-employed and work seasonally. Nursery and greenhouse workers grow plants from seeds to sell.

Something Extra

Are you happiest when you're outside? Does your perfect day involve sunshine, fresh air, and hard work? Do you like using your muscles and your mind together? If so, landscaping work may be just what you're looking for. These workers plant, prune, weed, and mow to make public areas beautiful. If your green thumb is your pride and joy, this may be the job for you.

Subjects to Study

Biology, zoology, botany, driver's education, business math

Discover More

Plant some flowers around your home or in a pot inside. Start with some easy annuals like snapdragons, petunias, or marigolds. Next, try something trickier, like orchids or roses. Can you make your flowers grow?

Related Jobs

Construction workers, landscape architects, farmers, horticultural workers, tree surgeon helpers, tree trimmers, pruners, and forest conservation workers

Short-term OJT to Bachelor's degree

Education & Training

$$–$$$

Earnings

Above-average increase

Job Outlook

Preschool Teachers & Child-Care Workers

On the Job

Preschool teachers and child-care workers care for children under the age of five. Those caring for infants and toddlers may change diapers, heat bottles, and rock children to sleep. Those caring for preschoolers serve meals, play games, read stories, and organize activities to help the children socialize and learn new skills. The work can be tiring, and workers must be strong enough to lift and move children. Some preschools are open only during the school year.

Subjects to Study

English, child development, psychology, home economics, art, music, drama, health, speech

Discover More

Visit a preschool and talk with the workers and children. What type of training do the workers have? The easiest way to learn about this job is to baby-sit or help someone else take care of preschoolers.

Related Jobs

Teacher aides, children's tutors, kindergarten and elementary school teachers, early childhood program directors, and child psychologists

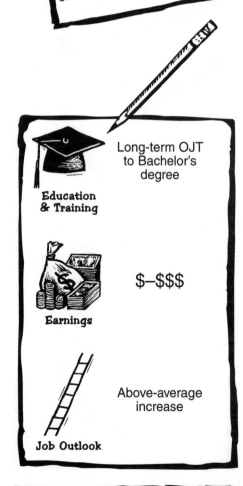

Education & Training
Long-term OJT to Bachelor's degree

Earnings
$–$$$

Job Outlook
Above-average increase

Private Household Workers

On the Job

Private household workers clean homes, care for children, cook meals, and do laundry. They may be companions for elderly or disabled people. Child-care workers and nannies care for and educate babies and young children. Housekeepers, butlers, caretakers, and cooks are other private household workers. These workers may live in their employers' homes, but most work days and return to their own homes at night.

Subjects to Study

Home economics, child care, first aid, cooking, shop courses

Discover More

A good way to learn about child care is to baby-sit for young children. If your school offers baby-sitting classes, sign up for one. Offer your services to neighbors and family friends with small children.

Related Jobs

Janitors and custodians, preschool teachers and child-care workers, home health aides, cooks, kitchen workers, waiters and waitresses, and bartenders

Short-term OJT

Education & Training

$

Earnings

Declining

Job Outlook

Veterinary Assistants & Nonfarm Animal Caretakers

On the Job

Animal caretakers feed, water, bathe, and exercise animals in clinics, kennels, and zoos. They play with the animals, watch them for illness or injury, and clean and repair their cages. Kennel staff care for cats and dogs; stable workers groom, exercise, and care for horses; and zookeepers care for wild and exotic animals. They may work outdoors in all kinds of weather. The work can be dirty and dangerous. Many work weekends and nights, and some travel with animals to sports events or shows.

Subjects to Study

Life sciences, zoology, biology, chemistry, physical education

Discover More

You can learn more about this occupation by volunteering at a zoo or animal shelter. You might play with or cuddle small animals, clean cages, put out food and water, or take animals for walks.

Related Jobs

Agricultural and biological scientists, veterinarians, retail sales workers in pet stores, gamekeepers, poultry breeders, ranchers, and artificial-breeding technicians

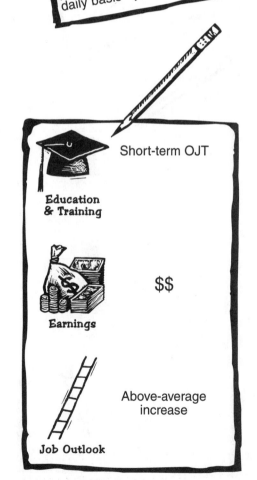

Education & Training
Short-term OJT

Earnings
$$

Job Outlook
Above-average increase

Correctional Officers

On the Job

Correctional officers guard people who are awaiting trial and those who have been convicted of crimes. They keep order and enforce rules in jails or prisons and assign and supervise inmates' work. They help inmates with personal problems and report any bad behavior. To prevent escapes, they stand guard in towers and at gates. They work indoors and outdoors under very stressful conditions. Many work nights and weekends. These workers must be strong and able to use firearms.

Something Extra

In the late 1700s, England used the colony of Australia as a huge prison. Convicted thieves and murderers boarded ships in England and sailed to Australia, 12,000 miles from home. Some prisoners mistakenly believed that the island country was connected to China and died trying to walk to freedom. Others tried to escape by sea and were never heard from again. Some of Australia's population today is descended from these exiles.

Subjects to Study

Physical education, driver's education, psychology, sociology

Discover More

Some state prisons give tours to the public or to school groups. Check to see if you can visit one to learn more about this job.

Related Jobs

Bailiffs, bodyguards, house or store detectives, security guards, police officers, probation and parole officers, and recreation leaders

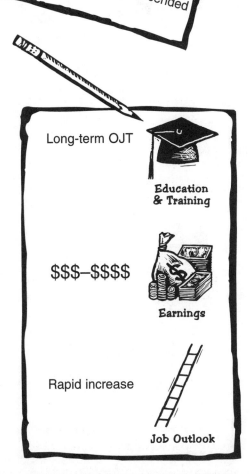

Long-term OJT

Education & Training

$$$–$$$$

Earnings

Rapid increase

Job Outlook

Firefighters

On the Job

Firefighters protect people from the dangers of fires. They must stay physically fit and strong. At the scene of a fire, they rescue victims, perform emergency medical aid, and operate and maintain equipment. During their shifts, firefighters live at the fire station. Most work 50 hours a week or more. Forest firefighters may parachute into a fire area to put out fires and dig a fire line. Fire-fighting is one of the most dangerous jobs in the U.S. economy.

Subjects to Study

Physical science, chemistry, driver's education, physical education

Discover More

Tour the fire station in your neighborhood or at your local airport. Ask the firefighters about their jobs, the training they receive, and the risks of the job.

Related Jobs

Fire-protection engineers, police officers, and emergency medical technicians

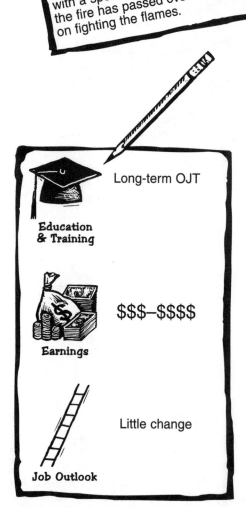

Education & Training
Long-term OJT

Earnings
$$$–$$$$

Job Outlook
Little change

Guards

On the Job

Guards protect property from fire, theft, vandalism, and break-ins. They patrol the area by walking, driving a car or motor scooter, or checking people entering and leaving the area. Guards usually wear uniforms and may carry a nightstick or gun. Most work some nights and weekends. They may work indoors or outdoors, and they must be able to stay calm in an emergency. The job can be lonely and dangerous.

Something Extra

Do people call you independent? Do you think of yourself as a loner? Security guards often work alone for hours at a time—especially those who work as night watchmen. To provide them with some protection, businesses sometimes give their night guards transmitters. The guards use these to maintain contact with a central station. If the guard does not check in at the expected times, or if he or she doesn't respond to a call, the station sends someone to check on him or her.

Subjects to Study

English, driver's education, physical education, communication skills, computer skills

Discover More

Call a security company in your area and ask if you can speak with someone who hires security guards. Ask that person about the skills you would need to be a guard. Does the company provide training?

Related Jobs

Bailiffs, border guards, correction officers, fish and game wardens, house or store detectives, police officers, and private investigators

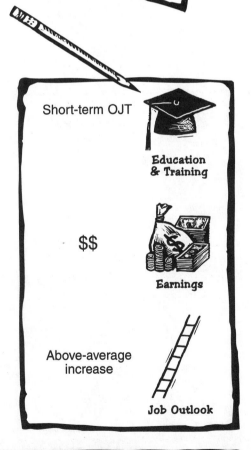

Short-term OJT

Education & Training

$$

Earnings

Above-average increase

Job Outlook

Police, Detectives, & Special Agents

On the Job

Police, detectives, and special agents protect people from crime and violence. They patrol highways, issue traffic tickets, and help accident victims. They also collect evidence and investigate crimes. Police detectives often testify in court about their cases. Most work some evenings and weekends. Police work is dangerous and stressful.

Subjects to Study

English, psychology, sociology, chemistry, physics, driver's education, physical education, foreign languages

Discover More

Police officers often check for fingerprints at the scene of a crime. Make your own fingerprinting kit with talcum powder, a paintbrush, and a magnifying glass. Dust the powder lightly on a solid, shiny surface like a doorknob. Blow gently. The powder will blow away, except where the greasy marks are. Brush the powdered spots lightly with the paintbrush, and examine the prints with the glass.

Related Jobs

Guards, bailiffs, correction officers, deputy sheriffs, fire marshals, fish and game wardens, and U.S. marshals

Education & Training
Long-term OJT to Bachelor's degree

Earnings
$$$–$$$$

Job Outlook
Average increase

Private Detectives & Investigators

On the Job

Private detectives and investigators work for lawyers, insurance companies, and other kinds of businesses. They gather information for trials, track down people who owe companies money, and conduct background checks. Some are self-employed and specialize in searching for missing persons or finding information for divorce cases. They may spend long hours watching a person or place, hunting for clues, and interviewing people. They often work irregular hours and travel, and the work may be dangerous.

Subjects to Study

English, psychology, sociology, chemistry, physics, driver's education, physical education, foreign languages

Discover More

An investigator's main job is collecting information. Use your investigative skills to find interesting information about this job. What can you find at the library or on the Internet that you didn't know before?

Related Jobs

Security guards, insurance claims investigators, inspectors, collectors, and law enforcement officers

Long-term OJT

Education & Training

$$$

Earnings

Above-average increase

Job Outlook

Mechanic, Installer, & Repairer Occupations

Aircraft Mechanics, Including Engine Specialists

Something Extra

Pilots and aircraft mechanics work together to maintain airplanes. When a pilot finds a problem before takeoff, he or she reports it to the mechanic. The mechanic checks the plane to find the cause of the problem and corrects it. The plane is repaired as quickly as possible so the flight can take off on time.

On the Job

Aircraft mechanics and engine specialists inspect airplanes for problems. They make repairs and test equipment to make sure it is working properly. Some mechanics work on several different types of planes while others specialize in just one type. Some mechanics even specialize in one part of an aircraft, such as the engine or electrical system of a DC-10. Sometimes they work inside, but often they work outdoors. Most mechanics wear earplugs to protect their hearing.

Subjects to Study

Math, physics, chemistry, electronics, computer science, mechanical drawing

Discover More

To find out more about aircraft mechanics, write to the Flight Safety Foundation, 601 Madison Street, Suite 300, Alexandria, VA 22314. Or visit its Web site at www.flightsafety.org.

Related Jobs

Electricians, elevator repairers, and telephone maintenance mechanics

Voc/tech training

Education & Training

$$$$

Earnings

Average increase

Job Outlook

Automotive Body Repairers

On the Job

Automotive body repairers fix cars and trucks damaged in accidents. They straighten bent bodies, hammer out dents, and replace parts that can't be fixed. Their supervisors usually decide what parts to fix, which ones to replace, and how long the job should take. In large shops, some repairers specialize in one type of repair, such as installing glass or repairing doors.

Something Extra

Did you know that some cars have parts made from plastic? If these parts are damaged, a body repairer can use heat from a hot-air welding gun or simply put the damaged part in very hot water to make the plastic soft. Then the repairer can mold the softened part into its original shape and put it back on the car.

Subjects to Study

Shop courses, automotive body repair, science courses, math

Discover More

A model car has many of the same body parts as a real car. Buy a model car kit and build and paint the model. Can you customize the car, so it reflects your personality?

Related Jobs

Automotive and diesel mechanics, automotive repair service estimators, and painters

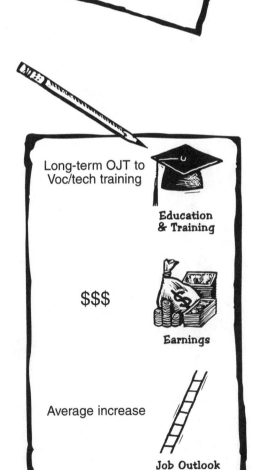

Long-term OJT to Voc/tech training

Education & Training

$$$

Earnings

Average increase

Job Outlook

Automotive Mechanics

On the Job

Automotive mechanics repair and service cars, trucks, and vans that have gas engines. Mechanics must be quick and accurate when they are diagnosing mechanical problems. During routine service work, mechanics inspect, adjust, and replace vehicle parts. They usually follow a checklist to make sure they examine parts that might cause a future breakdown. Some mechanics are self-employed.

Subjects to Study

Math, shop courses, automotive mechanics, electronics, physics, chemistry, computer skills

Discover More

Do you know someone who works on cars? Ask that person if you can help or just watch while he or she works on a car. You can learn a lot by watching and listening as a mechanic works. You might even be able to help by handing him or her tools.

Related Jobs

Diesel truck and bus mechanics, motorcycle mechanics, automotive body repairers, painters, and repair service estimators

Education & Training
Long-term OJT to Voc/tech training

Earnings
$$$$

Job Outlook
Average increase

Diesel Mechanics

On the Job

Diesel mechanics repair and maintain diesel engines in heavy trucks, buses, and other equipment like tractors, bulldozers, and cranes. They spend a lot of time doing preventive maintenance to make sure the equipment operates safely, to prevent wear and tear, and to reduce expensive breakdowns. Most work in repair shops, but some work outdoors to repair equipment at construction sites.

Something Extra

Diesel engines are heavier and last longer than gas engines. They're also more efficient because a diesel engine compresses its fuel—so it uses less to do more. This means that more fuel is available to power the engine. Large trucks, buses, trains, and even some cars have diesel engines these days.

But while diesel fuel is more efficient, it might be harder to find at your local gas station.

Subjects to Study

Math, shop courses, automotive repair, electronics, computer skills

Discover More

Do you know the differences between gas engines and diesel engines? You can find out by reading about engines and how they work. Check out some science books from the library and learn about both kinds of engines.

Related Jobs

Aircraft mechanics, automotive mechanics, boat engine mechanics, farm equipment mechanics, mobile heavy equipment mechanics, motorcycle mechanics, and small-engine specialists

Long-term OJT to Voc/tech training

Education & Training

$$$

Earnings

Little change to some increase

Job Outlook

Electronic Equipment Repairers

On the Job

Electronic equipment repairers install, repair, and maintain things like TVs, computers, telephones, and industrial equipment controls. Many of them work for telephone companies. Others work in homes, factories, offices, or hospitals. Some are self-employed, working from home or at their own repair shops. All of these workers keep detailed records of the work they do on each piece of equipment.

Subjects to Study

Math, physics, science courses, shop courses, electronics

Discover More

Visit a service center or repair shop. Talk to the repairers about their work. Ask how they became interested in the work and what kind of training they needed.

Related Jobs

Appliance and power tool repairers, automotive electricians, broadcast technicians, vending machine repairers, and electronics engineering technicians

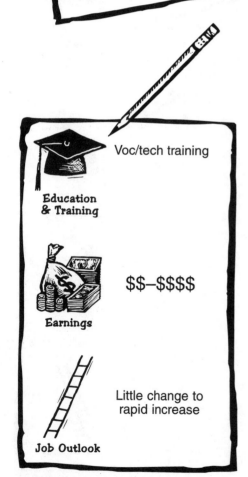

Education & Training
Voc/tech training

Earnings
$$–$$$$

Job Outlook
Little change to rapid increase

Commercial & Industrial Electronic Equipment Repairers

On the Job

These workers install and repair equipment in factories. About one-third of them work for the federal government, many for the Department of Defense. They install radar, missile controls, and communication systems on ships, aircraft, tanks, and in buildings. Other electronic equipment repairers work for telephone companies, hospitals, and in repair shops.

Something Extra

Since the first bands of nomads started arguing over territory, armies have been coming up with new ways to throw weapons at their enemies. During the Middle Ages, warriors used catapults to launch stones, dead horses, and even manure into enemy camps. Gunpowder and the first guns brought that kind of warfare to an end. Today's warriors use computers to guide missiles to their targets—which is a lot cleaner than loading manure onto a catapult!

Subjects to Study

Math, physics, science courses, shop courses, electronics

Discover More

You can work on electronics projects in a science club or 4-H club. Ask your teacher if one of these clubs meets at your school.

Related Jobs

Appliance and power tool repairers, automotive electricians, broadcast technicians, vending machine repairers, and electronics engineering technicians

Voc/tech training

Education & Training

$$$–$$$$

Earnings

Rapid increase

Job Outlook

Communications Equipment Repairers

On the Job

Communications equipment repairers install, repair, and maintain complex telephone equipment. Most work either in a phone company's central office or in the field at customers' homes or offices. Others work on equipment for cable TV companies, railroads, or airlines. Some work nights and weekends, and they may be on call to handle emergencies.

Subjects to Study

Math, science courses, shop courses, electronics, physics

Discover More

Take apart an old telephone and look at its insides. Can you follow the wires to their sources? Can you figure out what the different parts do? Now, can you put it back together?

Related Jobs

Appliance and power tool repairers, automotive electricians, broadcast technicians, electronic organ technicians, vending machine repairers, and electronics engineering technicians

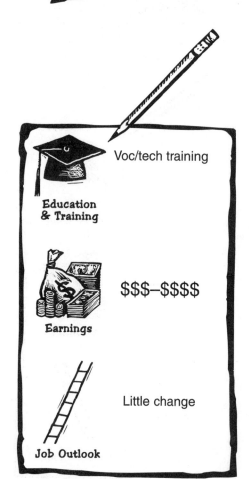

Education & Training — Voc/tech training

Earnings — $$$–$$$$

Job Outlook — Little change

Computer & Office Machine Repairers

On the Job

Computer repairers install and fix computers, equipment used with computers, and word processing systems. Office machine repairers work on copiers, typewriters, cash registers, and mailing equipment. Some repairers work on both computers and office equipment. These repairers work in many industries, and some are on call 24 hours a day to make emergency repairs.

Something Extra

Thomas Jefferson is famous for writing the Declaration of Independence, but did you know he was also an inventor? In fact, Jefferson invented the first copy machine. Here's how it worked. As the writer wrote a document, a second pen connected to a machine made another copy of the document. This way a writer could create two copies at once.

Subjects to Study

Math, computer science, physics, shop courses, electronics

Discover More

Do you know how to hook up a computer? Ask the teacher in your school's computer lab to show you how to connect a computer's cables to the printer or scanner.

Related Jobs

Appliance and power tool repairers, automotive electricians, broadcast technicians, vending machine repairers, and electronics engineering technicians

Long-term OJT to Voc/tech training

Education & Training

$$$

Earnings

Above-average increase

Job Outlook

Electronic Home Entertainment Equipment Repairers

On the Job

These repairers work on radios, TV sets, stereos, cameras, video games, and other home electronic equipment. They run tests to find problems and adjust and replace parts. They sometimes use complicated equipment to help them detect problems. Most work in repair shops or in service departments at larger stores. They may make home visits to fix equipment. Some are self-employed.

Subjects to Study

Math, science courses, shop courses, electronics, physics

Discover More

Visit a VCR repair shop in your area. Ask the technicians if you can watch as they make repairs and run tests.

Related Jobs

Appliance and power tool repairers, automotive electricians, broadcast technicians, vending machine repairers, and electronics engineering technicians

Education & Training
Long-term OJT to Voc/tech training

Earnings
$$$

Job Outlook
Declining

Telephone Installers & Repairers

On the Job

Telephone installers and repairers travel to people's homes and offices to install and repair telephones and other communication equipment. When customers move or ask for additional phone lines or other services, installers make the changes. They also install lines and telephone jacks in new buildings. Nearly all of these workers are employed by telephone companies.

Something Extra

People first began renting telephones to use in their businesses and homes in 1877. In those days, a phone at home was a luxury item. Today, 99% of homes in America have at least one phone, and many have two or more. We have phones in our cars, carry cellular phones in our purses and briefcases, and even take them with us to dinner and the movies.

Subjects to Study

Math, physics, shop courses, electronics

Discover More

You can find out more about careers in the telephone industry by writing for a copy of Phonefacts from the United States Telephone Association, Small Companies Division, 900 19th Street NW, Suite 800, Washington, DC 20006.

Related Jobs

Appliance and power tool repairers, automotive electricians, broadcast technicians, vending machine repairers, and electronics engineering technicians

Long-term OJT to Voc/tech training

Education & Training

$$$–$$$$

Earnings

Average increase

Job Outlook

Elevator Installers & Repairers

On the Job

Elevator installers and repairers assemble, install, repair, and replace elevators and escalators. They repair and update older equipment and install new equipment. They also test the equipment to make sure it works properly. These workers must have a thorough knowledge of electricity and electronics. They may be on call 24 hours a day to help out in an emergency.

Subjects to Study

Math, shop courses, science courses, electronics, physics, first aid

Discover More

Learn about apprenticeship programs by visiting the Elevator Constructors' Union Web site at http://job.careernet.org/elevate.htm.

Related Jobs

Boilermakers, electricians, industrial machinery repairers, millwrights, sheet-metal workers, and structural ironworkers

Education & Training
Short-term OJT

Earnings
$$$$

Job Outlook
Little change to some increase

Farm Equipment Mechanics

On the Job

Farm equipment mechanics repair all kinds of farm machinery including tractors, combines, planters, hay balers, and milking machines. They keep machinery in good working order by tuning, cleaning, and adjusting engines and checking for problems. Repairing farm equipment can be seasonal work. These workers might work seven days a week during planting and harvesting seasons, but be unemployed during the winter.

Something Extra

In some parts of the United States, people known as *the Amish* do not use any modern mechanical or electrical equipment on their farms. Instead, they use horses to pull their plows and work the soil. But the Amish, along with other small farmers, are being squeezed out of farming because of big, factory-style farms. As a result, many Amish farmers have become construction workers instead.

Subjects to Study

Vocational courses, diesel and gas engines, hydraulics, welding, electronics

Discover More

Visit a farm, a farm equipment show, or a state fair. Ask the people working with the equipment to explain how it is used on modern farms.

Related Jobs

Aircraft mechanics, automotive mechanics, diesel mechanics, and mobile heavy equipment mechanics

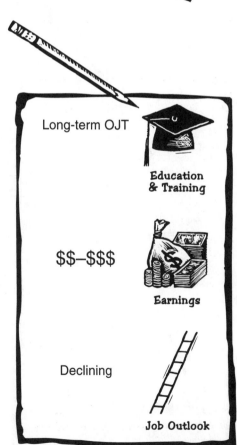

Long-term OJT

Education & Training

$$–$$$

Earnings

Declining

Job Outlook

General Maintenance Mechanics

On the Job

General maintenance mechanics have a lot of variety in their work, so they need many different skills to do their jobs. They use plumbing, electrical, painting, and carpentry skills in their work. These workers maintain equipment in hospitals, stores, offices, and other businesses. In a small business, they might do all of the repairs. In a larger organization, they might be responsible for one specific area.

Subjects to Study

Math, shop courses, mechanical drawing, electronics, woodworking, blueprint reading, science courses

Discover More

Try your hand at assembling a clock. Ask your parents if they have an old alarm clock you can take apart, or get an inexpensive one at the drugstore. Use a screwdriver to remove the back and take it apart. Make sure it's not plugged in!

Related Jobs

Carpenters, plumbers, industrial machinery mechanics, electricians, and air-conditioning, refrigeration, and heating mechanics

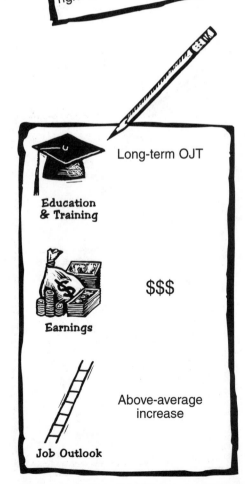

Education & Training

Long-term OJT

Earnings

$$$

Job Outlook

Above-average increase

Heating, Air-Conditioning, & Refrigeration Technicians

On the Job

These technicians help keep people comfortable by installing and repairing heating systems and air conditioners. They also help protect food and medicine that must be kept refrigerated. These workers maintain, diagnose, and correct problems within entire heating or cooling systems. They may work for large companies or be self-employed.

Subjects to Study

Shop courses, math, electronics, mechanical drawing, physics, chemistry, blueprint reading, physical education

Discover More

Visit your local supermarket and ask to talk with someone who works in the frozen food or dairy section. Ask how repairs are made to the cooling systems.

Related Jobs

Boilermakers, electrical appliance repairers, electricians, plumbers, pipe fitters, and sheet-metal workers

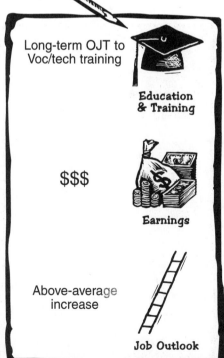

Long-term OJT to Voc/tech training

Education & Training

$$$

Earnings

Above-average increase

Job Outlook

Home Appliance & Power Tool Repairers

On the Job

These workers repair ovens, washers, dryers, refrigerators, and other home appliances. They also repair power tools such as saws and drills. First, they find the problem. Then they replace or repair faulty parts. At the same time, they tighten, clean, and adjust other parts if needed. They must keep good records, prepare bills, and collect payments.

Subjects to Study

Shop courses, electronics, math, science courses

Discover More

Call a repair shop in your area and ask if you can help in the shop for a day or two. Watch how the repairer works and help out by bringing tools, waiting on customers, or cleaning the shop.

Related Jobs

Heating, air-conditioning, and refrigeration mechanics, office machine repairers, electronic home entertainment equipment repairers, and vending machine repairers

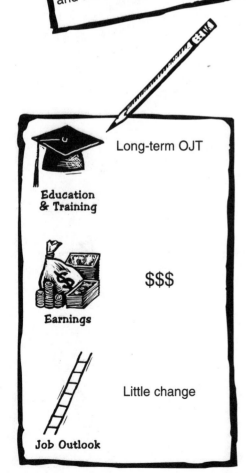

Education & Training — Long-term OJT

Earnings — $$$

Job Outlook — Little change

Industrial Machinery Repairers

On the Job

Industrial machinery repairers maintain machines in factories or plants to keep the work on schedule. Their work includes keeping machines and their parts oiled, tuned, and cleaned. When repairs are needed, the repairer must work quickly so production is not delayed, which might cause the company to lose money. Sometimes this means making emergency repairs at night or on weekends.

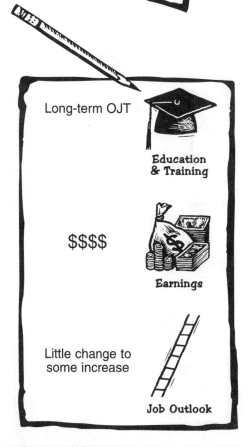

Something Extra

Industrial machine repairers must be able to spot and fix little problems before they cause major breakdowns. If a machine has a vibration that shouldn't be there, mechanics must find the source of the problem, such as a worn belt or loose bearing. The more repairs they make at early stages, the more money they save their employers down the road. After all, it's a lot cheaper to replace a worn belt than to repair an engine damaged by one.

Subjects to Study

Mechanical drawing, math, blueprint reading, science courses, physics, electronics, physical education, computer skills

Discover More

Contact the office of a factory in your area and ask for a tour. Watch the machinery used in production. Ask your guide what would happen to the production schedule if an important piece of machinery broke down.

Related Jobs

Aircraft mechanics, engine specialists, automotive mechanics, diesel mechanics, machinists, general maintenance mechanics, millwrights, and mobile heavy equipment mechanics

Long-term OJT

Education & Training

$$$$

Earnings

Little change to some increase

Job Outlook

Line Installers & Cable Splicers

On the Job

Line installers and cable splicers lay the wires and cables that bring electricity, phone service, and cable TV signals into our homes. They clear lines of tree limbs, check them for damage, and make emergency repairs when needed. This job can be dangerous because installers and splicers work underground, high above ground, and with various chemicals and electricity.

Subjects to Study

Math, physical education, shop courses, science, electronics

Discover More

Contact the human resource department of your local electric company, telephone company, or cable TV company. Ask about the kinds of jobs they have and what kind of training they require.

Related Jobs

Communication equipment mechanics, telephone installers and repairers, electricians, and sound technicians

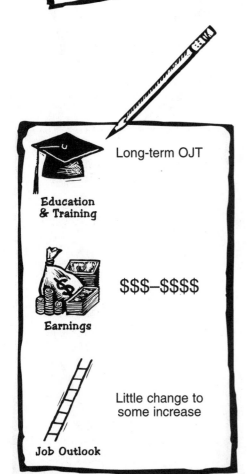

Education & Training — Long-term OJT

Earnings — $$$–$$$$

Job Outlook — Little change to some increase

Millwrights

On the Job

Millwrights work with machinery and heavy equipment. They take equipment apart and put it back together. They also oversee and supervise workers who load and unload equipment. They maintain machinery to avoid breakdowns. Most work outdoors at least some of the time, and they may be on call 24 hours a day to help in emergencies.

Something Extra

Millwrights work with many different types of equipment. One day they might be asked to move a huge printing press from one plant to another. Another day, they might take apart an X-ray machine in a clinic and rebuild it in a hospital. These workers must know the best ways to move all kinds of equipment. They also must know how much weight ropes, cables, hoists, and cranes can hold.

Subjects to Study

Science, math, mechanical drawing, shop courses, physical education

Discover More

Visit the library and find a book that explains pulley systems. Think of a job that could be made easier using pulleys. Then ask a teacher to help you build an experimental pulley for that purpose.

Related Jobs

Industrial machinery repairers, mobile heavy equipment mechanics, aircraft mechanics, diesel mechanics, farm equipment mechanics, ironworkers, and machine assemblers

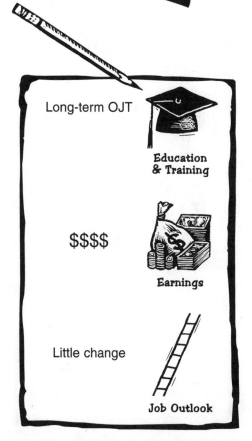

Long-term OJT

Education & Training

$$$$

Earnings

Little change

Job Outlook

Mobile Heavy Equipment Mechanics

Something Extra

When a big piece of machinery breaks down at a logging site or a mine, the workers can't simply pack it up and bring it into the repair shop. That's where a field service mechanic comes in. These workers drive specially equipped trucks to the work site to make the repair. They may be on the job for a week or two before they're off to the next site. Many mechanics enjoy the independence of working outside the repair shop.

On the Job

Mobile heavy equipment mechanics repair the machinery used in construction, logging, and mining. They fix and maintain motor graders, trenchers, backhoes, bulldozers, and cranes. They service and repair diesel engines and other machine parts. They may also repair the hydraulic lifts used to raise and lower scoops and shovels. These workers are outdoors in all kinds of weather.

Subjects to Study

Math, automobile mechanics, science courses, physics, chemistry

Discover More

Visit a construction site and watch how the equipment moves and works. Talk to a construction worker about what happens when a machine breaks down.

Related Jobs

Rail car repairers, diesel, farm equipment, and mine machinery mechanics

Education & Training
Long-term OJT to Voc/tech training

Earnings
$$$–$$$$

Job Outlook
Little change to some increase

Motorcycle, Boat, & Small-Engine Mechanics

On the Job

Motorcycle, boat, and small-engine mechanics do routine engine checkups and repair everything from chain saws to yachts. The mechanic first talks with the owner to try to understand the problem. Then he or she runs tests to find the source of the problem. In some areas, mechanics may work much more during the summer than they do in the winter. Many of these workers are self-employed.

Something Extra

If you take a job in a restaurant, you wouldn't expect to bring your own pots and pans, would you? But mechanics often must provide their own hand tools for their work.

Most beginning mechanics start out with the basics, like wrenches, pliers, screwdrivers, and power drills. As they gain experience, they collect more tools. Experienced mechanics may have thousands of dollars invested in tools.

Subjects to Study

Business math, small-engine repair, shop courses, science, electronics

Discover More

Ask your parents or neighbor if you can help them prepare their lawnmower for spring use or winter storage. As you work, ask about the various parts of the motor.

Related Jobs

Automotive mechanics, diesel mechanics, farm equipment mechanics, and mobile heavy equipment mechanics

Long-term OJT to Voc/tech training

Education & Training

$$–$$$

Earnings

Little change to some increase

Job Outlook

Musical Instrument Repairers & Tuners

Something Extra

A piano tuner's tools include pliers, wire cutters, and various kinds of scrapers. Using a tuning fork, the tuner tightens or loosens the "A" string until it sounds like the tuning fork. Then he or she sets the pitch of each of the 230 strings in relation to that "A" string. Tuning a piano takes about an hour and a half and requires a good ear.

On the Job

Musical instrument repairers and tuners usually specialize in one kind of instrument. They may work for instrument stores or be self-employed. Piano tuners often travel to people's homes to do their jobs. Organ repairers also travel, usually to churches, to make repairs on huge pipe organs. Other repairers may work in the store or repair shop. They restring guitars and violins, re-cover drums, or replace valves on brass instruments. Some are self-employed.

Subjects to Study

Woodworking, instrumental music, communication skills, business math

Discover More

Talk to your school's music teacher or band director about how to care for instruments. Volunteer to help care for the instruments at your school.

Related Jobs

Electronic home entertainment equipment repairers, vending machine repairers, home appliance and power tool repairers, and computer and office machine repairers

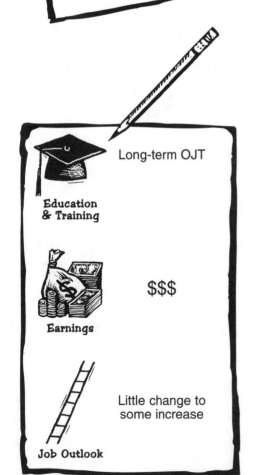

Education & Training
Long-term OJT

Earnings
$$$

Job Outlook
Little change to some increase

Vending Machine Servicers & Repairers

On the Job

Vending machine servicers and repairers check coin-operated machines that offer entertainment, soft drinks, snacks, sandwiches, and other items for sale. They retrieve money, stock the machines, and make sure the machines are clean and working properly. They also keep records and order parts. These workers travel from place to place to make repairs. They may be outside in all kinds of weather.

Subjects to Study

Driver's education, shop courses, electronics, machine repairs, math

Discover More

The next time you see someone servicing a vending machine, stop and talk with him or her. Ask about the best and worst parts of the job. How much time does the repairer spend on the road?

Related Jobs

Home appliance and power tool repairers, electronic equipment repairers, and general maintenance mechanics

Long-term OJT

Education & Training

$$$

Earnings

Little change to some decline

Job Outlook

Construction Trades Occupations

Bricklayers & Stonemasons

On the Job

Bricklayers and stonemasons lay sidewalks and patios, build fireplaces, and install ornamental exteriors on buildings. Bricklayers work with concrete blocks, firebrick linings in furnaces, and brick. Stonemasons work with natural and artificial stones. They often build walls on churches, office buildings, and hotels. Bricklayers and stonemasons work outdoors in all types of weather. They must be strong enough to move heavy materials. Many are self-employed.

Subjects to Study

Business math, mechanical drawing, shop courses, art, physical education

Discover More

You can learn more about brick and stonework training programs by checking out the International Masonry Institute's Web site at www.imiweb.org. Or call the Institute at 1-800-562-7464.

Related Jobs

Concrete masons and terrazzo workers, tile setters, and plasterers

Education & Training — Long-term OJT

Earnings — $$$$

Job Outlook — Average increase

Carpenters

On the Job

Carpenters do all kinds of construction work, including woodworking, concrete work, drywall work, and many other jobs. They replace doors, windows, and locks; repair wooden furniture; hang kitchen cabinets; and install machinery. They work with hand and power tools and read blueprints. Carpenters form the largest group of building trade workers. Most work in new construction or remodeling. Others are self-employed.

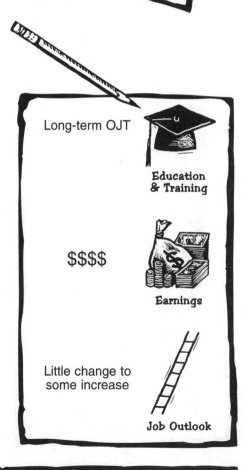

Something Extra

In the past, carpentry was a family trade. Boys were taught by their fathers, who had been taught by their fathers before them. Skills and tools were handed down from one generation to the next. Some carpenters still learn the trade from their fathers or grandfathers, but today most learn by taking woodworking classes and becoming apprentices.

Subjects to Study

Shop courses, mechanical drawing, carpentry, business math, first aid

Discover More

Try a simple carpentry project such as building a doghouse, a shelf, or a flower box. First, get a plan and gather the materials you need. Be sure you know how to use your tools safely before you begin.

Related Jobs

Bricklayers, concrete masons and terrazzo workers, electricians, pipe fitters, plasterers, plumbers, and stone masons

Long-term OJT

Education & Training

$$$$

Earnings

Little change to some increase

Job Outlook

Carpet Installers

On the Job

Carpet installers put carpet in new or old buildings and houses. First, they check the existing floor for any needed repairs or problems. Then they measure the floor and plan the carpet layout. They stretch the carpet to make it fit snugly before they attach it to a stripping, which holds it in place. Most work regular daytime hours, but some work evenings. These workers spend their days kneeling, bending, stretching, and lifting heavy rolls of carpet.

Subjects to Study

Shop courses, driver's education, physical education, business math

Discover More

Carpet installers must measure rooms precisely. Using a tape measure and a calculator, measure a room in your house. Include nooks, bends, and closets. Take the total width of the room and multiply by the total length to get the square footage.

Related Jobs

Carpenters, cement masons and terrazzo workers, drywall workers, lathers, painters and paperhangers, roofers, sheet-metal workers, and tile setters

Education & Training — Short-term OJT

Earnings — $$$–$$$$

Job Outlook — Average increase

Concrete Masons & Terrazzo Workers

On the Job

Concrete masons use a mixture of cement, gravel, sand, and water to build home patios, huge dams, and miles of roads. They pour the concrete and smooth the finished surface. Terrazzo workers add marble chips to the surface of concrete to create decorative walls, sidewalks, and panels. These workers spend their days outdoors, bending, stooping, and kneeling. Most wear kneepads and water-repellent boots for protection.

Something Extra

Have you ever heard the expression, "All roads lead to Rome"? The ancient Romans took their road building seriously. Only Roman men of the highest rank were allowed to build and maintain the roads. At the height of the Roman Empire, 29 different roads led from Rome to the farthest stretches of the empire, to Northern Europe and the Middle East and even into parts of Africa. Those cement-block roads were so well-constructed they have lasted for more than 2,000 years.

Subjects to Study

Shop courses, blueprint reading, mechanical drawing, driver's education, physical education, business math

Discover More

The International Masonry Institute offers terrazzo training to apprentices and journeymen. Check out its Web site at www.imiweb.org. Or call the Institute at 1-800-562-7464.

Related Jobs

Bricklayers, form builders, marble setters, plasterers, stonemasons, and tile setters

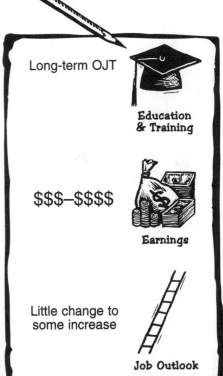

Long-term OJT

Education & Training

$$$–$$$$

Earnings

Little change to some increase

Job Outlook

Drywall Workers & Lathers

On the Job

In most buildings, the walls and ceilings are made of drywall. Drywall workers fasten drywall panels to a building's framework. Then they fill the joints between boards and prepare the wall for decorating. Lathers put metal or gypsum lath on walls, ceilings, and frameworks for support. These workers spend their days standing, reaching, and bending. They work on ladders and high scaffolding and wear masks so they don't breathe in the dust from their work. Many are self-employed.

Subjects to Study

Shop courses, carpentry, physical education, business math

Discover More

Visit a hardware store or lumberyard and look at the drywall pieces. Ask the sales workers how the boards are cut and what tools drywallers use.

Related Jobs

Carpenters, carpet installers, insulation workers, and plasterers

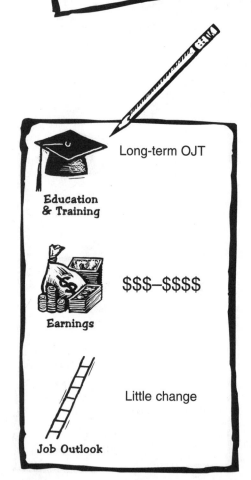

Education & Training
Long-term OJT

Earnings
$$$–$$$$

Job Outlook
Little change

Electricians

On the Job

Electricians work with the systems that provide electricity to homes and businesses. They may install wiring, heating, and air-conditioning systems, or make repairs to such systems. They must follow government rules and building codes to ensure their safety and the safety of the buildings they work on. Electricians may work nights and weekends and be on call 24 hours a day. Many are self-employed.

Subjects to Study

Math, shop courses, electronics, mechanical drawing, science, blueprint reading, first aid

Discover More

Can you get power from a lemon? Try this experiment using a strip of copper, a strip of zinc, a small flashlight bulb, and a lemon. Insert the metal strips into the lemon, close together but not touching. Now put the end of the lightbulb on the zinc and the end of the copper on the threads. The acid in the lemon should make the bulb light up.

Related Jobs

Air-conditioning mechanics, cable installers and repairers, electronics mechanics, and elevator repairers

Long-term OJT to Voc/tech training

Education & Training

$$$$

Earnings

Little change to some increase

Job Outlook

Glaziers

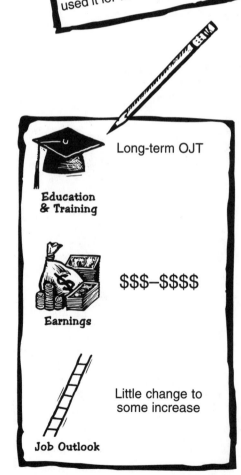

Long-term OJT

Education & Training

$$$–$$$$

Earnings

Little change to some increase

Job Outlook

On the Job

Glaziers cut, install, and remove all kinds of glass and plastics in doors, windows, showers, and baths. They often use glass that is precut and mounted in a frame. They may use cranes to lift large, heavy pieces into place. Once the glass is mounted, glaziers secure it with bolts, cement, metal clips, or wood molding. Glaziers work outdoors in all kinds of weather. They sometimes work on ladders and high scaffolding.

Subjects to Study

Shop courses, business math, blueprint reading, mechanical drawing, general construction, first aid

Discover More

Make your own "stained glass" creation by getting a window-hanger kit from your local craft store. These kits contain metal frames and small, colored beads. You simply fill the frame with beads, then put it in the oven to melt the beads so that they look like glass.

Related Jobs

Bricklayers, carpenters, carpet installers, paperhangers, terrazzo workers, and tile setters

Insulation Workers

On the Job

Builders put insulation in buildings to save energy by keeping the heat in during the winter and the heat out during the summer. Insulation workers cement, staple, wire, tape, or spray insulation between the inner and outer walls or under the roof of a building. They often use a hose or blowing machine to spray a liquid insulation that dries into place. These workers must wear protective suits, masks, and respirators. They work on ladders and in dusty, dirty areas. Many are self-employed.

Something Extra

Have you ever heard of asbestos? It's a material that was once widely used for insulation in homes and buildings across America. It is fire-resistant and very effective. Unfortunately, it also causes cancer in people exposed to it.

Insulation workers who deal with asbestos must wear special protective clothing, gloves, and masks to prevent asbestos contamination. This safety clothing keeps them safe from cancer.

Subjects to Study

Shop courses, blueprint reading, general construction, physical education, driver's education

Discover More

Head to your local hardware store and check out the different kinds of insulation. Ask the sales worker about each kind. Ask your parents what kind of insulation your home has. If you live in an apartment building, ask the building manager.

Related Jobs

Carpenters, carpet installers, drywall workers, roofers, sheet-metal workers

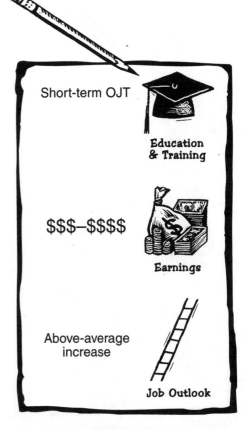

Short-term OJT

Education & Training

$$$–$$$$

Earnings

Above-average increase

Job Outlook

Painters & Paperhangers

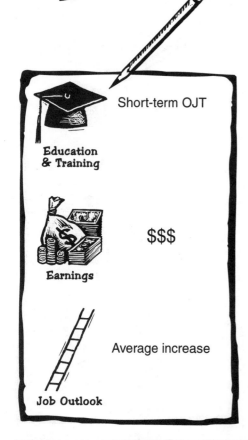

Education & Training

Short-term OJT

Earnings

$$$

Job Outlook

Average increase

On the Job

Painters and paperhangers make inside walls look clean, attractive, and bright by applying decorative paint or wallpaper to them. They also paint outside walls with special paints that protect the walls from weather damage. Painters mix paints to match colors, then brush and roll the paints onto surfaces.

Sometimes they rag-roll, splatter, or sponge on a second coat of paint in a different color. Paperhangers apply sizing and wallpapers and add decorative borders. Many are self-employed and work outdoors or seasonally.

Subjects to Study

Shop courses, art courses, business math, art, physical education

Discover More

Try your painting skills by refinishing an old piece of furniture. First, sand off the old finishing, then clean the surface completely. Apply two or three even coats of a new color, then coat the surface with a clear finish.

Related Jobs

Billboard posterers, metal sprayers, undercoaters, and transportation equipment painters

Plasterers

On the Job

Plasterers apply plaster to walls and ceilings to make them fire-resistant and more soundproof. They also apply insulation to the outside of new or old buildings. They create smooth or textured finishes using trowels and combs. Skilled plasterers sometimes specialize in complicated decorative work. Many are self-employed. Plasterers may work outdoors or indoors. The work is physically demanding. Some of the materials they use may irritate the eyes and skin.

Something Extra

Say the word *plaster,* and you might think of walls or ceilings, but do you think of swimming pools? Well, maybe you should. Many contractors use plaster as a pool coating because it can stand up to the chemicals commonly used in pool water. It is durable and easy to clean, and it is nontoxic and easy on the environment. So the next time you take a dip in the pool, check out the bottom. Is it plaster?

Subjects to Study

Mechanical drawing, shop courses, art, drafting, blueprint reading, physical education, business math

Discover More

Make garden stones for your home or school. Mix plaster of paris and pour it into a flat, round mold. Place marbles, beads, and small shells in patterns in the wet plaster. Allow the plaster to dry, then remove the mold.

Related Jobs

Drywall workers, bricklayers, concrete masons and terrazzo workers, marble setters, stonemasons, and tile setters

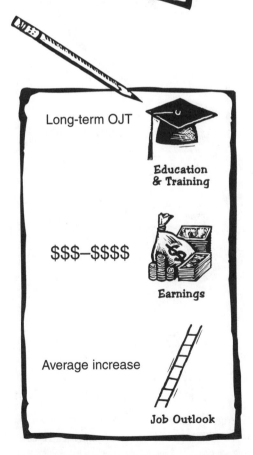

Long-term OJT

Education & Training

$$$–$$$$

Earnings

Average increase

Job Outlook

Plumbers & Pipe Fitters

On the Job

Plumbers install and repair water, waste disposal, drainage, and gas pipe systems in homes and other buildings. They also install showers, sinks, toilets, and appliances. Pipe fitters install and repair the pipe systems used in manufacturing, creating electricity and heating and cooling buildings. These workers may work nights and weekends, or be on call 24 hours a day. They must be strong enough to lift heavy pipes. Many are self-employed.

Subjects to Study

Shop courses, drafting, blueprint reading, physics, physical education, business math

Discover More

Tour your home or school and look at the pipe work in the bathrooms and kitchen. Are the pipes lead, stainless steel, or copper? Are the joints taped or welded? Are there other kinds of piping in the building?

Related Jobs

Boilermakers, stationary engineers, electricians, elevator installers, industrial machinery repairers, millwrights, sheet-metal workers, and heating, air-conditioning, and refrigeration workers

Education & Training
Long-term OJT to Voc/tech training

Earnings
$$$$

Job Outlook
Little change

Roofers

On the Job

Roofers install roofs made of tar or asphalt and gravel, rubber, metal, and other materials. They may install or repair the tiles on private home roofs, or repair old roofs on other buildings. Some also waterproof concrete walls and floors. These workers do physically demanding work outdoors, including lifting, climbing, and stooping. They risk injury from slips, falls, and burns. The roofing industry has the highest accident rate of all construction work.

Subjects to Study

Shop courses, mechanical drawing, physical education, business math

Discover More

Make a survey of roofing materials in your neighborhood. How many houses and buildings have asphalt-shingled roofs? Are there any buildings in your area with metal roofs or wooden shingles?

Related Jobs

Carpenters, concrete masons and terrazzo workers, drywall workers, plasterers, and tile setters

Something Extra

In the 1970s, James Taylor recorded a song called "Up on the Roof." In it, Taylor sang about escaping from the worries of the world and sitting on the rooftop, just relaxing.

In reality, rooftops can be steep, slippery, scary places. They're not a good place for daydreaming, and roofing is not a good job for those who are careless or afraid of heights. In fact, roofers have the highest accident rate of all the construction trades.

Short-term OJT

Education & Training

$$$

Earnings

Little change

Job Outlook

Sheet-Metal Workers

On the Job

Sheet-metal workers use large sheets of metal to make ductwork for air-conditioning and heating systems. They also make roofs, rain gutters, skylights, outdoor signs, and other products. They install and maintain these products as well. They usually work in shops or at the job site. They must be strong enough to lift heavy, bulky items. They wear safety glasses to protect their eyes, and they cannot wear jewelry or loose-fitting clothing around the machinery they use.

Subjects to Study

Algebra, geometry, mechanical drawing, shop courses, physical education

Discover More

To learn more about this job, write to the Sheet Metal National Training Fund, 601 N. Fairfax St., Suite 240, Alexandria, VA 22314.

Related Jobs

Machinists, metal fabricators, metal pattern makers, shipfitters, tool and die makers, glaziers, and heating, air-conditioning, and refrigeration workers

Education & Training
Short- to Long-term OJT

Earnings
$$$–$$$$

Job Outlook
Little change

Structural & Reinforcing Ironworkers

On the Job

These workers build the steel frames used to strengthen bridges, high-rise buildings, highways, and other structures. They install metal stairways, window frames, decorative ironwork, and other metal products. Some erect metal storage tanks and other premade buildings.

Structural and reinforcing ironworkers work outdoors in extremely high places, on scaffolding and beams. They must be strong enough to lift heavy pieces of metal.

Something Extra

It took 8,000 tons of steel, 93,167 high-strength bolts, and a 250-ton crane to build a 5,000-foot drawbridge. All that and just 15 people. That's right, a crew of 14 ironworkers and one crane operator built the bridge that connected the cities of Portland and South Portland, Maine. In only two months they laid almost 1,000 feet of girders. Which just goes to show, experienced ironworkers can accomplish almost anything!

Subjects to Study

Shop courses, mechanical drawing, blueprint reading, business math, physical education

Discover More

You can learn more about the physics of bridge-building by making your own bridge. Stack four books in two piles that are the same height, four inches apart. Now use an index card as a bridge between the stacks. How many pennies can you put on the card before the "bridge" collapses? Now move the books closer and arch your bridge. Will it hold more pennies?

Related Jobs

Operating engineers, concrete masons, and welders

Long-term OJT

Education & Training

$$$$

Earnings

Little change to some increase

Job Outlook

Tile Setters

On the Job

Tile setters use cement or a sticky paste called *mastik* to set tiles on walls, floors, or ceilings. They arrange tiles in decorative patterns, and cut them to fit into corners and around fixtures. Once the tiles are set, they fill the joints around them with a fine cement called grout. Tile setters usually work indoors, but they spend much of the workday bending, kneeling, and reaching. Many wear kneepads to protect their knees.

Subjects to Study

Mechanical drawing, shop courses, blueprint reading, art, physical education, business math

Discover More

Head to your local craft shop to get a mosaic-making kit—either one with a premade design or one you can design yourself. Cut the tiles as needed, then arrange them into a pattern of your choice.

Related Jobs

Bricklayers, concrete masons and terrazzo workers, plasterers, stone masons, and marble workers

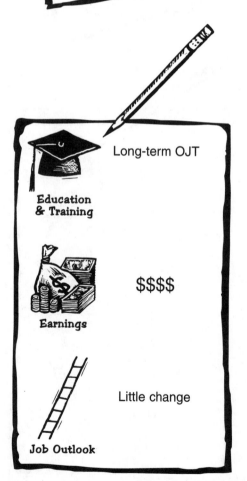

Education & Training — Long-term OJT

Earnings — $$$$

Job Outlook — Little change

Factory & Production Occupations

Precision Assemblers

On the Job

Precision assemblers are experienced and trained workers who put together complicated products like computers, appliances, and electronic equipment. Their work is detailed and must be done accurately. They follow directions from engineers and use several tools and precise measuring instruments. Some work in clean, well-lit, dust-free rooms, while others work around grease, oil, and noise. They may have to lift and fit heavy objects.

Subjects to Study

Math, science, computer education, shop courses, electronics

Discover More

Get a kit from an electronics store and assemble a radio or another piece of electronic equipment.

Related Jobs

Welders, ophthalmic laboratory technicians, and machine operators

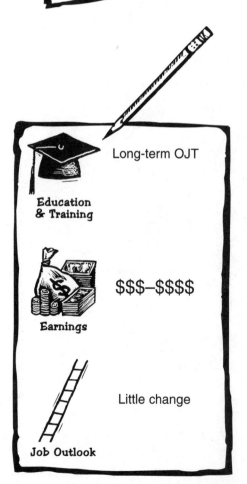

Education & Training
Long-term OJT

Earnings
$$$–$$$$

Job Outlook
Little change

Blue-Collar Worker Supervisors

On the Job

Blue-collar worker supervisors are in charge of groups of workers in a factory or at a construction site. They make work schedules, oversee workers, check machinery, and train new employees. They are often in charge of expensive equipment or systems. A supervisor's main responsibility is making sure that work gets done. Supervisors may work day, evening, or night shifts, indoors or outdoors, holidays and weekends.

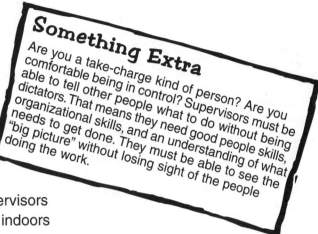

Something Extra

Are you a take-charge kind of person? Are you comfortable being in control? Supervisors must be able to tell other people what to do without being dictators. That means they need good people skills, organizational skills, and an understanding of what needs to get done. They must be able to see the "big picture" without losing sight of the people doing the work.

Subjects to Study

Math, English, communication skills, speech, psychology, shop courses

Discover More

Volunteer to be a team leader for a school project. You will delegate jobs to other workers, help them as needed with their jobs, and make sure all the work gets done right and on time.

Related Jobs

Retail store or department managers, clerical supervisors, bank officers, head tellers, hotel managers, postmasters, head cooks, head nurses, and surveyors

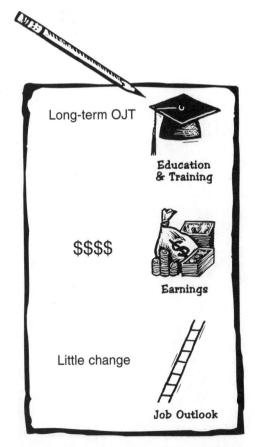

Long-term OJT

Education & Training

$$$$

Earnings

Little change

Job Outlook

Fishers, Hunters, & Trappers

On the Job

Fishers catch fish and sea animals in rivers, lakes, and at sea. Hunters track and kill animals for government agencies or to sell. They may hunt alone, with others, or with dogs. Trappers catch animals using traps or cages and sometimes sell wild animal skins. All these workers spend most of the time outdoors, sometimes in dangerous situations. The hours are long and the work is hard.

Subjects to Study

Physical education, mechanics, business math, first aid

Discover More

You can learn about living outdoors in a program like the Girl Scouts or Boy Scouts or through an outdoor education program at the YMCA.

Related Jobs

Zookeepers, loggers, animal control officers, forest rangers, fishing guides, game wardens, harbor pilots, and wildlife management specialists

Education & Training
Short-term OJT

Earnings
$$

Job Outlook
Little change to some decline

Forestry & Logging Workers

On the Job

Forestry and conservation workers help develop and protect forests by planting new trees, fighting the pests and diseases that attack trees, and helping to control soil erosion. Timber cutters and loggers cut down thousands of acres of forests each year for the timber that is used for wood and paper products. Forestry and logging workers work outdoors in all kinds of weather. Their work is demanding and dangerous.

Something Extra

Sometimes a job has its own language that is foreign to outsiders. For example, if you spent time with logging workers, you'd hear some different job titles.

Fallers and buckers cut down trees. Choker setters fasten chokers (steel chains) around logs to be skidded (dragged) by tractors to the landing. And riggers set up and dismantle the cables and guide wires on the logs.

Subjects to Study

Physical education, first aid, mechanics

Discover More

Learn to identify the different kinds of trees in your area. Study a tree identification book and then visit a forest or park. How many trees can you identify?

Related Jobs

Arborists, gardeners, groundskeepers, landscapers, nursery workers, range aides, and soil conservation technicians

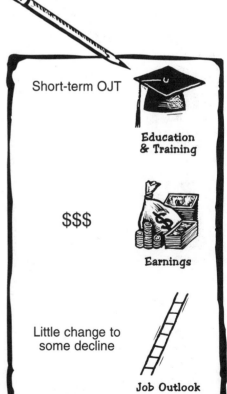

Short-term OJT

Education & Training

$$$

Earnings

Little change to some decline

Job Outlook

Butchers & Meat, Poultry, & Fish Cutters

On the Job

Butchers and meat, poultry, and fish cutters cut animal meat into small pieces to be sold to customers. They remove bones from certain cuts of meat, and remove inedible parts such as the head, tail, and scales of fish.

They may work in a small market, in a large refrigerated room, or on an assembly line. Their work areas must be clean, but they are often cold and damp. These workers have the highest rate of work-related injuries and illnesses of any industry.

Subjects to Study

Health, nutrition, home economics, food preparation

Discover More

Learn about the different cuts of meat, fish, and poultry. Visit the meat department of a grocery store near you to see the different cuts. Talk to the butcher and ask about the job.

Related Jobs

Bakers, chefs, cooks, and food preparation workers

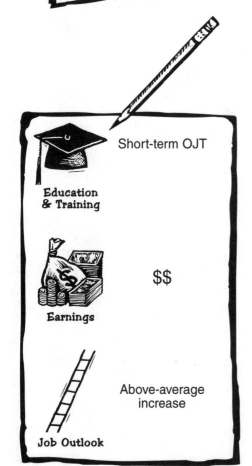

Education & Training — Short-term OJT

Earnings — $$

Job Outlook — Above-average increase

Inspectors, Testers, & Graders

On the Job

Inspectors, testers, and graders examine products before releasing them to consumers. They may test by looking, listening, feeling, tasting, or smelling. Products must meet certain quality standards. Inspectors may reject a product, send it back to be fixed, or fix the problem themselves. Inspectors work in all kinds of industries. Some move from place to place. Others sit on an assembly line all day.

Something Extra

How does a toy company ensure that each toy it produces is well-made and safe for children? It hires inspectors to test them. A toy inspector might poke, pull, and drop a toy to see if it breaks or measure it to see if it might be a choking hazard for young children.
Inspectors work in every industry that produces an item for sale.

Subjects to Study

English, math, shop courses, blueprint reading, mechanics

Discover More

Learn how to contact a company if you are not satisfied with a product. Check the packaging of some products in your home for a consumer telephone number or an address.

Related Jobs

Construction and building inspectors, and compliance officers, except construction

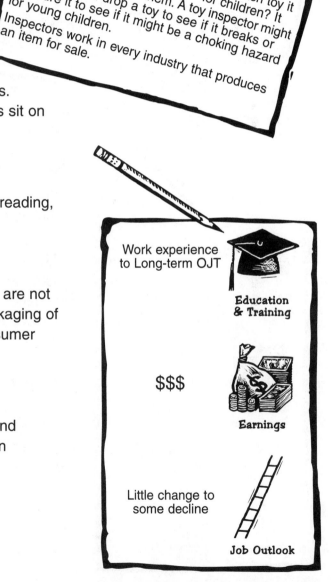

Work experience to Long-term OJT

Education & Training

$$$

Earnings

Little change to some decline

Job Outlook

Boilermakers

On the Job

Boilermakers build boilers, vats, and other large tanks used for storing liquids and gases. Boilers supply steam for electric engines and for heating and power systems in buildings, factories, and ships. Because most boilers last for 35 years or more, repairing and maintaining them is a big part of a boilermaker's job. These workers use dangerous equipment, lift heavy items, and may work on ladders or scaffolding.

Subjects to Study

Math, shop courses, blueprint reading, welding, machine metalworking

Discover More

Most boilermakers belong to labor unions. Find out what labor unions are active in your community. Contact one and ask about what the union does and how people become members.

Related Jobs

Assemblers, blacksmiths, instrument makers, ironworkers, machinists, millwrights, pattern makers, plumbers, sheet-metal workers, tool and die makers, and welders

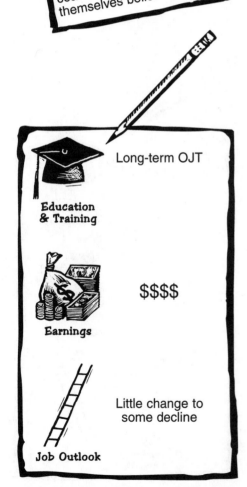

Education & Training
Long-term OJT

Earnings
$$$$

Job Outlook
Little change to some decline

Jewelers

On the Job

Jewelers use precious metals and stones such as gold and diamonds to make necklaces, rings, bracelets, and other jewelry. Some specialize in one area, such as buying, designing, cutting, repairing, selling, or appraising jewels. This work requires a high degree of skill and attention to detail. Jewelers use chemicals, sawing and drilling tools, and torches in their work. Some are self-employed.

Subjects to Study

Math, art, mechanical drawing, chemistry, computer skills, blueprint reading

Discover More

Take a jewelry-making class at school or your local craft store. Try designing and selling your own jewelry pieces.

Related Jobs

Polishers, dental laboratory technicians, gem cutters, hand engravers, and watchmakers and repairers

Something Extra

One of the most famous jewels in the world is the Hope Diamond. This 45½-carat blue diamond was found in the early 1600s and has crossed oceans and continents and passed from kings to commoners. It has been stolen and recovered, sold and resold, cut and recut.

But its fame is due to the bad luck it seems to bring its owners. More than 20 deaths have been blamed on the gem. Through the years its owners have been killed by wild dogs, beheaded, and committed suicide.

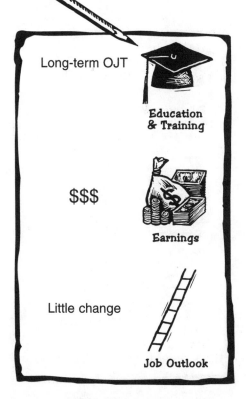

Long-term OJT

Education & Training

$$$

Earnings

Little change

Job Outlook

Machinists & Tool Programmers

Something Extra

What does a company do when it needs a special part for its one-of-a-kind machine? It hires a machinist to make the part. Machinists make everything from huge metal pincers to tiny metal bits—whatever the client needs. Some machinists even work making copies of antique tools and machinery for living museums and collectors. They use today's technologies to re-create yesterday's tools.

On the Job

Machinists make metal parts using lathes, drill presses, and milling machines. They often make specialized parts or one-of-a-kind items. Most work in machine shops and wear safety glasses and earplugs. Tool programmers specialize in computer programming to make parts. A computer gives instructions to a machine that follows each step until the part is done. Tool programmers often work in an office near the machine shop.

Subjects to Study

Math, shop courses, blueprint reading, drafting, physics, mechanical drawing, computer skills, electronics

Discover More

Visit a machine shop in your community. High school shops and vocational schools are some places you can find metalworking machines. Ask the instructor to show you how the machines work.

Related Jobs

Tool and die makers, tool planners, instrument makers, blacksmiths, gunsmiths, locksmiths, metal pattern makers, and welders

Education & Training
Long-term OJT to Voc/tech training

Earnings
$$$$

Job Outlook
Little change to some increase

Metalworking & Plastics-Working Machine Operators

On the Job

Think of how many products today are made of metal and plastic parts. The workers who produce these parts are separated into two groups: those who set up the machines and those who tend the machines during production. These powerful, high-speed machines can be dangerous. Workers wear safety glasses and earplugs for protection.

Something Extra

One growing part of the plastics field is recovery and recycling. Many communities now offer curbside pickup of recyclable materials like paper and plastic.
To recycle plastic, the handler first sorts and cleans the items, then shreds them into flakes or chops them into pellets. These flakes and pellets are then formed into new plastic items—everything from bottles and clothes to car parts and toys.

Subjects to Study

Math, shop courses, blueprint reading, first aid

Discover More

Many plastic products today are made from recycled plastic. This is good for the environment and for the economy. Start a recycling program in your neighborhood or at your school.

Related Jobs

Machinists, tool and die makers, extruding and forming machine operators, woodworking machine operators, and metal pattern makers

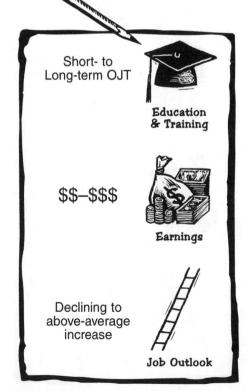

Short- to Long-term OJT

Education & Training

$$-$$$

Earnings

Declining to above-average increase

Job Outlook

Tool & Die Makers

On the Job

Tool and die makers are highly skilled workers. Toolmakers create tools that cut, shape, and form metal and other materials. Die makers make dies, which are the forms used to shape metal in stamping and forging machines. Tool and die makers must know about machining operations, mathematics, and blueprint reading. They must follow safety rules and wear protective clothing on the job. They spend a good part of the day standing and must be able to lift heavy items.

Subjects to Study

Math, shop courses, blueprint reading, metalworking, drafting, machine shop, mechanical drawing

Discover More

Using pen and paper, design a new tool to do something useful. Or think up a new use for an old tool. Can you convert an egg slicer to cut bagel chips?

Related Jobs

Machinists, mold makers, instrument makers, metal-making machine operators, tool programmers, blacksmiths, gunsmiths, locksmiths, metal pattern makers, and welders

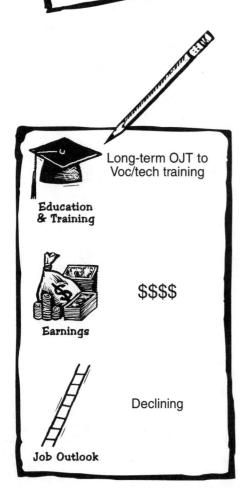

Education & Training
Long-term OJT to Voc/tech training

Earnings
$$$$

Job Outlook
Declining

Welders, Cutters, & Welding Machine Operators

On the Job

Welders use the heat from a torch to permanently join metal parts together. Because of its strength, welding is used to build ships, cars, aircraft, and even the space shuttle. Welders may use a hand torch or a welding machine. They also use torches to cut and dismantle metal objects. Welders must wear protective gear to prevent burns and injuries. Some work outdoors on ladders or scaffolding.

Subjects to Study

Shop courses, blueprint reading, shop math, mechanical drawing, physics, chemistry

Discover More

To learn more about this occupation, write to the American Welding Society, 550 N.W. LeJeune Rd., Miami, FL 33126-5699.

Related Jobs

Blacksmiths, forge shop workers, machinists, machine-tool operators, tool and die makers, millwrights, sheet-metal workers, boilermakers, and metal sculptors

Something Extra

Say the word welder, and many people think of a guy in a hard hat and goggles. But many of today's welders are women, and they can trace their history to the shipyards of World War II. During the war, the shipyards of San Francisco were so short of workers they began hiring and training housewives and mothers to do jobs traditionally held by men. These "lady welders" in overalls even had a popular song written and named for them: "Rosie the Riveter."

Long-term OJT to Voc/tech training

Education & Training

$$$

Earnings

Little change

Job Outlook

Electric Power Generating Plant Operators & Power Distributors & Dispatchers

On the Job

Electric power plant operators control the machinery that generates electricity. They start or stop generators as power requirements change. Power distributors and dispatchers make sure that users receive enough electricity. They plan for times when more electricity is needed and handle emergencies. These workers often work nights, weekends, and holidays.

Subjects to Study

Math, physics, electronics, computer science, shop courses, English

Discover More

Talk to someone at the public relations department of your local electric company. Find out where your electricity is generated. Can you take a field trip to see the plant?

Related Jobs

Stationary engineers, water and sewage treatment plant operators, waterworks pump-station operators, chemical operators, and refinery operators

Education & Training
Long-term OJT

Earnings
$$$$

Job Outlook
Little change to some increase

Stationary Engineers

On the Job

Stationary engineers operate and maintain equipment that provides air-conditioning, heat, and ventilation to large buildings. This equipment may supply electricity, steam, or other types of power. These workers may work weekends and holidays. They are exposed to heat, dust, dirt, and noise from the equipment. Hazards of the job include burns, electric shock, and injury from moving machinery parts.

Something Extra

One of the largest power plants in the U.S. is at the Hoover Dam on the Colorado River. With 17 generators, the plant provides low-cost power to cities and towns in Nevada, Arizona, and California—enough power to serve 1.3 million people.

The dam was built in the 1930s, during the Great Depression, as part of a federal program that created jobs for the unemployed.

Subjects to Study

Math, computer science, mechanical drawing, shop courses, chemistry, physical education

Discover More

Learn how to maintain and care for machines in your home such as the lawnmower and electric tools. Learn what tools to use, how to oil the machines, and how to keep them in good repair.

Related Jobs

Nuclear reactor operators, power station operators, water and wastewater treatment plant operators, waterworks pump-station operators, chemical operators, and refinery operators

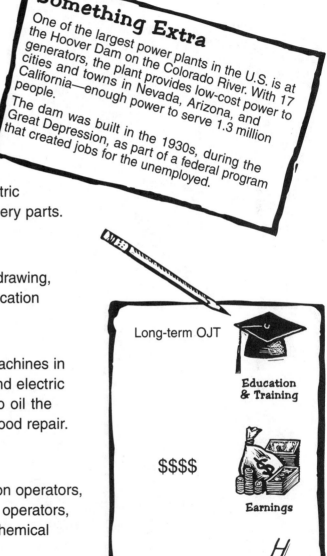

Long-term OJT

Education & Training

$$$$

Earnings

Declining

Job Outlook

Water & Wastewater Treatment Plant Operators

On the Job

Water treatment plant operators make sure that the water you drink is safe. Wastewater plant operators remove harmful pollution from wastewater. These workers read meters and gauges and adjust controls. They take water samples, perform analyses, and test and adjust chemicals in the water, such as chlorine. They work both indoors and outdoors and may be exposed to dangerous gases. They may work day, evening, or night shifts, weekends, and holidays.

Subjects to Study

Math, chemistry, biology, shop courses, health, environmental sciences

Discover More

Call the water company in your community and ask if your class can participate in a water-testing program. Many companies will send a representative to your school to teach a class on how to test the water at school and in your home for pollutants like lead and harmful bacteria.

Related Jobs

Boiler operators, power plant operators, power reactor operators, stationary engineers, chemical plant operators, and petroleum refinery operators

Education & Training
Long-term OJT

Earnings
$$$–$$$$

Job Outlook
Above-average increase

Bindery Workers

On the Job

Bindery workers use machines to "bind" the pages of books and magazines together in a cover. These machines fold, cut, gather, glue, stitch, sew, trim, and wrap pages to form a book. Bindery work is physically hard. Workers stand, kneel, lift, and carry heavy items. Many work on assembly lines. Some work in hand binderies, and a few are self-employed.

Something Extra

Did you know that some rare old books are worth thousands of dollars? So what does a library or museum do when one of these treasures starts to fall apart? They call in a bookbinder. These workers use special tools and chemicals to restore pages. Then they rebind the book by hand, using needle and thread.

Subjects to Study

Math, English, art, history, shop courses

Discover More

Bind your own book. First make an "end paper" by folding a sheet of heavy paper over your pages. Sew the pages into the end paper, using a heavy thread and needle. Paste each end paper to a heavy cardboard square. Now paste the squares onto a sheet of wallpaper. Cut the wallpaper to leave one inch of trim. Fold the trim over the cardboard squares and paste them down.

Related Jobs

Paper-making machine operators, press workers, and precision machine operators

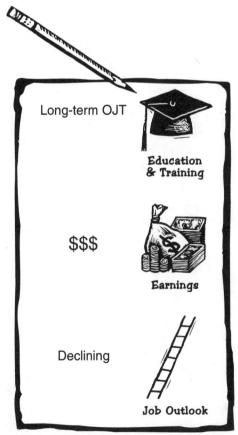

Long-term OJT

Education & Training

$$$

Earnings

Declining

Job Outlook

Prepress Workers

On the Job

Prepress workers prepare materials for printing presses. They do typesetting, design page layouts, take photographs, and make printing plates. With personal computers, customers can now show workers how they want their printed material to look. Prepress workers have different titles depending on their jobs. Most work at video monitors, and some work with harmful chemicals.

Subjects to Study

English, writing skills, electronics, computer skills, art, photography, typing

Discover More

Learn how to use word processing and graphics programs on a computer. Industry standards include Microsoft Word®, Corel's WordPerfect®, Adobe's PageMaker® and Photoshop®, and Quark®. Design your own greeting card or brochure.

Related Jobs

Sign painters, jewelers, decorators, engravers, graphic artists, computer terminal system operators, and keypunch operators

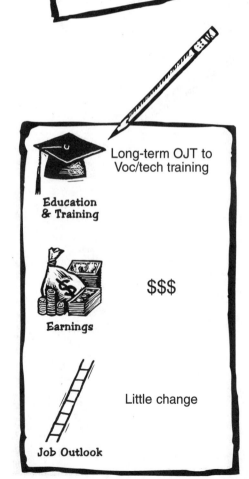

Education & Training
Long-term OJT to Voc/tech training

Earnings
$$$

Job Outlook
Little change

Printing Press Operators

On the Job

Printing press operators prepare, operate, and maintain the printing presses in a pressroom. They check the paper and ink, make sure paper feeders are stocked, and monitor the presses as they are running. Computerized presses allow operators to make adjustments at a control panel by simply pressing buttons. These workers are on their feet most of the time. The work can be physically hard. Most wear earplugs around the presses.

Something Extra

Before the Middle Ages, only a handful of people could read. That's because manuscripts had to be copied by hand. A group of workers called scribes were employed by monasteries to copy books. It was a time-consuming and expensive process. When a man named Gutenberg made the first printing press in 1456, he put a lot of scribes out of work. But he made books available to the common man for the first time in history.

Subjects to Study

Math, English, communication skills, computer science, chemistry, electronics, physics

Discover More

Try printing your own greeting cards with a wood-block printing kit. These kits are available at craft and hobby stores.

Related Jobs

Paper-making machine operators, shoe-making machine operators, bindery machine operators, and precision machine operators

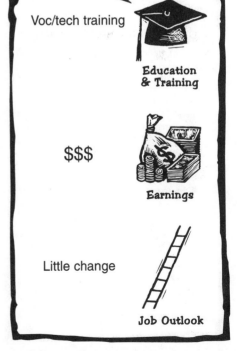

Voc/tech training

Education & Training

$$$

Earnings

Little change

Job Outlook

Apparel Workers

On the Job

Apparel workers make cloth, leather, and fur into clothing and other products. Many care for and clean these products. They may also repair torn or damaged items, or resew them to fit a customer better. Custom tailors make entire garments based on a customer's measurements.

Most apparel workers use sewing machines, but some do hand work. Some work in hot, noisy, crowded workshops, while others work in retail stores and bridal shops.

Subjects to Study

Home economics, sewing, computer skills, art

Discover More

Get a pattern for a simple sewing project. Follow the pattern directions to make something you can wear.

Related Jobs

Metalworking and plastics-working machine operators, textile machine operators, precision woodworkers, precision assemblers, shoe and leather workers, upholsterers, and tool and die makers

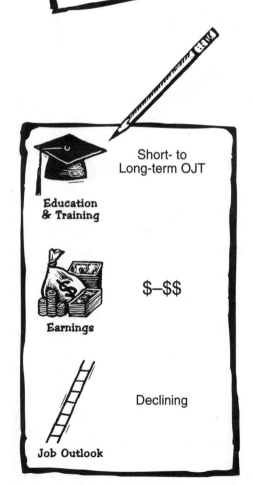

Education & Training

Short- to Long-term OJT

Earnings

$–$$

Job Outlook

Declining

Shoe & Leather Workers & Repairers

On the Job

Shoe and leather workers cut leather using patterns. Then they put the pieces together to make shoes, horse saddles, jackets, and luggage. Repairers fix worn leather shoes by attaching new heels and soles. They also resew seams and replace handles and linings on suitcases and handbags. They may work in noisy, crowded factories or in repair shops. Many shoe repairers are self-employed.

Something Extra

Before shoemaking machinery was widely used, shoemakers called *journeymen* traveled from house to house hawking their skills. The journeymen used the family's leather to make a year's supply of shoes for the entire family. They also repaired old shoes. When all the families in a town had shoes, the journeyman traveled to the next town to start over again.

Subjects to Study

Shop courses, sewing, home economics, art, business math

Discover More

You can learn more about working with leather by getting a leather-working kit from your local craft store. Follow the directions to make an item you can use.

Related Jobs

Dressmakers, designers, pattern makers, and furriers

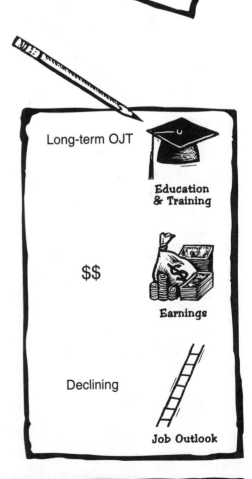

Long-term OJT

Education & Training

$$

Earnings

Declining

Job Outlook

Textile Machinery Operators

On the Job

Textile machinery operators care for and operate the machines that make textile goods. These goods are then used in all kinds of products, from clothing to materials in tires. Workers use machines that prepare fibers for spinning, make yarn, and produce fabric. They make sure the machines have yarn, repair breaks in the yarn, and repair the machines as needed. They may work day or evening shifts. Most wear protective glasses and masks.

Subjects to Study

English, shop courses, computer skills

Discover More

You can learn about weaving by getting a weaving kit from your local craft store. Most have a small frame, bands of fabric, and directions for making small items like pot holders.

Related Jobs

Extruding and forming machine operators, textile bleaching and dyeing machine operators, metal fabrication and plastics manufacturing operators

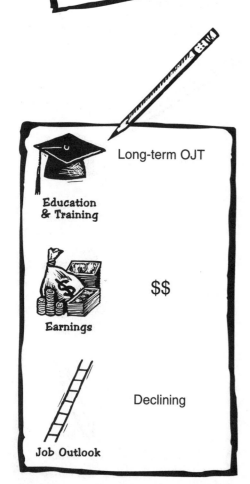

Education & Training — Long-term OJT

Earnings — $$

Job Outlook — Declining

Upholsterers

On the Job

Upholsterers are skilled craft workers who make new furniture or repair old furniture. They order supplies and help customers choose coverings. They use staple guns, pliers, shears, sewing machines, and special needles and threads to attach the coverings to the frames of furniture like chairs and couches. These workers stand most of the day and do a lot of bending and heavy lifting.

Something Extra

What do you do with an old couch—one that's looking shabby but still has a good frame? You could trash it, of course. But replacing it could cost a lot of money. Or you could take it to an upholsterer.

These workers can repair tears in the old fabric or re-cover your couch in all new fabric. This gives your old couch a new look and a new life, and it might save you a whole lot of money.

Subjects to Study

Home economics, sewing, upholstery, shop courses, woodworking, art, business math

Discover More

To learn more about this occupation, talk to an upholsterer or write to the Upholstery and Allied Industries Division, United Steelworkers of America, Local 18, 5320 W. North Avenue, Chicago, IL 60639.

Related Jobs

Fur cutters, furniture finishers, pattern and model makers, webbing tackers, and casket coverers

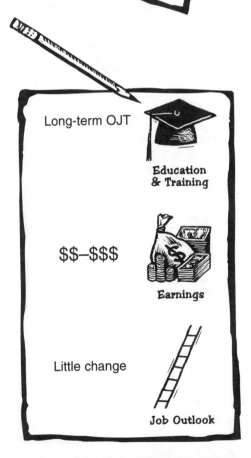

Long-term OJT

Education & Training

$$–$$$

Earnings

Little change

Job Outlook

Woodworkers

On the Job

Woodworkers make things from wood and work in many stages of the production process. They use machines that cut, shape, assemble, and finish wood to make doors, cabinets, paneling, and furniture. Precision woodworkers use hand tools to make rare or customized items. Most woodworkers handle heavy materials, stand for long periods, and risk exposure to dust and air pollutants. Some operate dangerous equipment.

Subjects to Study

Math, science, computer skills, shop courses, woodworking, blueprint reading, mechanics

Discover More

Ask an adult to help you with a woodworking project, such as building a shelf or a wooden toy.

Related Jobs

Precision metalworkers, metalworking and plastics-working machine operators, metal fabricators, molders and shapers, and leather workers

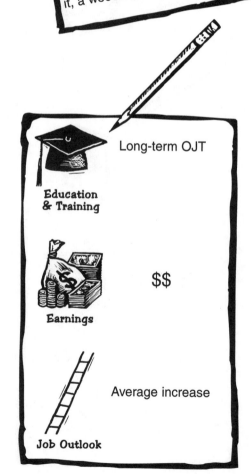

Education & Training — Long-term OJT

Earnings — $$

Job Outlook — Average increase

Dental Laboratory Technicians

On the Job

Dental laboratory technicians make the products dentists use to replace decayed teeth. Using dentists' directions and molds of patients' mouths, they make dentures (false teeth), crowns, and bridges. These workers usually have their own workbenches in clean, well-lit areas. Their work is very delicate and takes a lot of time. Salaried technicians usually work 40 hours a week, but self-employed technicians often work longer hours.

Subjects to Study

Sciences, art, metal and wood shop, drafting, business math, management courses

Discover More

Invite an orthodontist to speak to your class. Ask how he or she decides when someone needs braces, how to measure the patient's mouth, and how the braces are made.

Related Jobs

Arch-support technicians, orthotics technicians, prosthetics technicians, opticians, and ophthalmic laboratory technicians

Something Extra

What did people do before they had porcelain dentures? You've probably heard that George Washington had wooden teeth. But did you know that when Elizabeth I was queen of England (1558–1603), she lost all her front teeth to decay? To make her face appear fuller, Elizabeth put pieces of cloth under her lips. Other members of the royal court had ornamental teeth made from silver or gold.

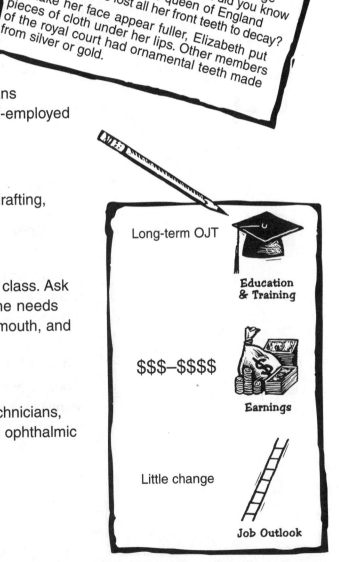

Long-term OJT

Education & Training

$$$–$$$$

Earnings

Little change

Job Outlook

Ophthalmic Laboratory Technicians

On the Job

Ophthalmic laboratory technicians make the lenses for eyeglasses. Some make lenses for instruments like telescopes and binoculars. They read the directions from eye doctors and mark the lenses to know where to grind the curves. Then they polish the lenses to remove the rough edges and put them in frames. They wear goggles to protect their own eyes while grinding the glass for lenses.

Subjects to Study

Math, science, English, shop courses, art

Discover More

Visit an optical store at your local mall. Most have ophthalmic labs on site. Ask if you can watch the technician work on a pair of glasses. Try on some frames while you're there.

Related Jobs

Biomedical equipment technicians, dental laboratory technicians, orthodontic technicians, prosthetics technicians, and instrument repairers

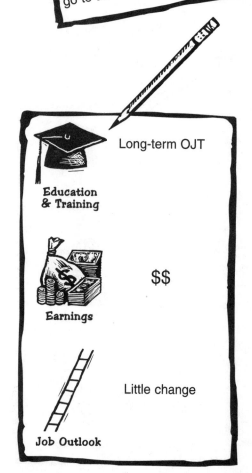

Education & Training — Long-term OJT

Earnings — $$

Job Outlook — Little change

Painting & Coating Machine Operators

On the Job

Painting and coating machine operators cover everything from cars to candy with paints, plastics, varnishes, chocolates, or special solutions. The most common methods of applying paints and coatings are spraying and dipping. These workers must wear respirators over their noses and mouths to protect themselves from dangerous fumes. Most work in factories, but self-employed car painters may own their own shops.

Something Extra

You probably can think of things that are painted—cars, toys, bikes, and wicker furniture. But what does a coating machine do? Well, paper coating machines spray the glossy finish on paper products. Silvering applicators spray a mix of silver, copper, and tin onto glass to make mirrors. And enrobing machines coat bakery goods with melted chocolate, sugar, or cheese.

Subjects to Study

Shop courses, art

Discover More

An auto body repair shop is one place you can watch spray painting in action. Call a shop and ask if you can watch the painters. You will probably have to watch from a distance because of the fumes.

Related Jobs

Construction and maintenance painters, electrolytic metal platers, painters, and decorators

Long-term OJT

Education & Training

$$

Earnings

Little change to some increase

Job Outlook

Photographic Process Workers

On the Job

Photographic process workers develop film, make picture prints and slides, and enlarge and retouch photographs. They also restore damaged and faded photographs. Most of these workers operate machines to complete their tasks. They are exposed to chemicals and must wear gloves and aprons for protection. Some work in large labs, while others work in one-hour mini-labs.

Subjects to Study

Math, art, computer science, photography

Discover More

Does your school have a darkroom? If so, find out who develops the photos for the school newspaper and yearbook. Ask if you can watch them do their work.

Related Jobs

Chemical laboratory technicians, crime laboratory analysts, food testers, medical laboratory assistants, quality control technicians, and engravers

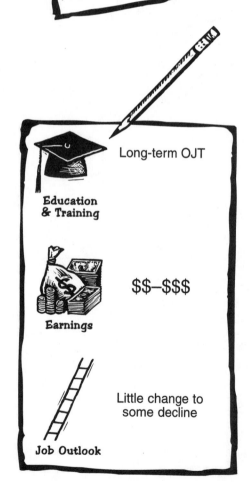

Education & Training
Long-term OJT

Earnings
$$–$$$

Job Outlook
Little change to some decline

Transportation & Material Moving Occupations

Bus Drivers

On the Job

Bus drivers transport people from place to place following a time schedule and a specific route. Some drive people long distances within a state or throughout the country. Others drive only locally. School bus drivers drive students to and from school. These workers deal with heavy traffic and many passengers, often in bad weather. Some work nights, weekends, and holidays; others travel overnight away from their homes. Many school bus drivers work part-time.

Subjects to Study

English, communication skills, math, driver's training, first aid

Discover More

Take a ride on a city bus and talk to the bus driver about this job. What tests does your state require? Is special training required? Watch what the driver does to communicate with passengers and care for the bus.

Related Jobs

Taxi drivers, truck drivers, and chauffeurs

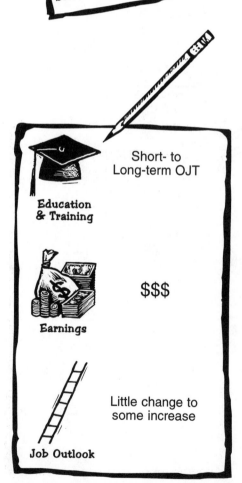

Short- to Long-term OJT

Education & Training

$$$

Earnings

Little change to some increase

Job Outlook

Material Moving Equipment Operators

On the Job

Material moving equipment operators load and unload trucks and ships using cranes, bulldozers, and forklifts. They move construction materials, logs, and coal around factories, warehouses, and construction sites. They sometimes set up, clean, and repair equipment. Most work outdoors in all kinds of weather. Others work inside warehouses or factories. The machinery may be noisy and dangerous.

Something Extra

Crane safety is a big concern today. That's because there are so many cranes operating on construction sites around the country, and they can be very dangerous equipment. In 1989, a tower crane collapsed in downtown San Francisco, killing two people. And in 1993 a mobile crane accident near Las Vegas killed three more. That's why cranes are inspected regularly, and operators receive special safety training.

Subjects to Study

Shop classes, auto mechanics, driver's education, first aid

Discover More

Look for material moving machines in your community. What do they move? Are they used in any work except construction? How do the operators control the machines?

Related Jobs

Truck drivers, bus drivers, manufacturing equipment operators, and farmers

Long-term OJT

Education & Training

$$$

Earnings

Little change

Job Outlook

Rail Transportation Workers

On the Job

This job includes railroad workers as well as subway and streetcar operators. Railroad engineers operate locomotives that transport passengers and cargo. Conductors are responsible for the cargo and passengers on trains. Brakemen remove cars and throw switches to allow trains to change tracks. Railroads operate around the clock, seven days a week. Employees work nights, weekends, and holidays. Some spend several nights a week away from home.

Subjects to Study

Math, mechanics, geography, driver's education, physical education

Discover More

Visit a railroad station or ride a train or subway and watch the different workers.

Related Jobs

Truck drivers, taxi drivers, and bus drivers

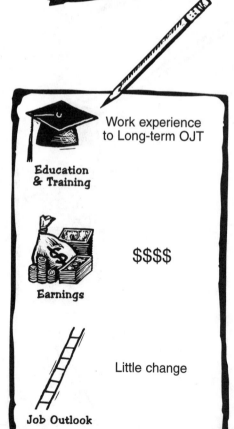

Education & Training
Work experience to Long-term OJT

Earnings
$$$$

Job Outlook
Little change

Taxi Drivers & Chauffeurs

On the Job

Taxi drivers and chauffeurs drive people in cars, limousines, and vans. Taxi drivers drive people to airports, hotels, or restaurants. Chauffeurs pamper their passengers by providing extras like newspapers, drinks, music, and television. These workers must lift heavy luggage and packages, drive in all kinds of weather and traffic, and sometimes put up with rude customers. Most taxi drivers and chauffeurs work nights and weekends.

Something Extra

Are you a night owl? Do you love to be on the road? If so, being a chauffeur may be just your ticket. Chauffeurs working for limousine companies often drive at night. They take people to concerts and parties, to dances and clubs, and sometimes to weddings. Many chauffeurs tell stories of driving famous folks in town for concerts or plays. Who knows? You could pick up your favorite actor at the airport and get an autograph along with a fare!

Subjects to Study

English, business math, physical education, driver's education

Discover More

Take a taxi ride and talk to the driver. Ask about the best and worst parts of the job. Has he or she ever driven anyone famous?

Related Jobs

Ambulance drivers, bus drivers, and truck drivers

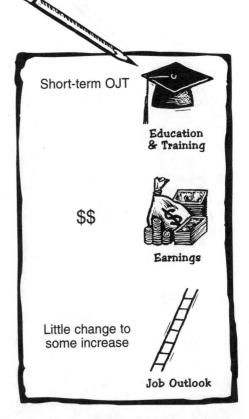

Short-term OJT

Education & Training

$$

Earnings

Little change to some increase

Job Outlook

Truck Drivers

On the Job

Truck drivers move and deliver goods between factories, terminals, warehouses, stores, and homes. They maintain their trucks, check for fuel and oil, make sure their brakes and lights work, and make minor repairs. They also load and unload the goods they transport. They drive in heavy traffic and bad weather. Some self-employed truckers may spend 240 days a year on the road.

Subjects to Study

Business math, driver's education, physical education, accounting

Discover More

Call a truck-driver training school in your area. Ask if you can visit the school and see the rigs they drive. Maybe an instructor will take you for a ride.

Related Jobs

Ambulance drivers, bus drivers, chauffeurs, and taxi drivers

Education & Training — Short-term OJT

Earnings — $$$

Job Outlook — Average increase

Water Transportation Workers

On the Job

Workers in water transportation use all kinds of boats on oceans, the Great Lakes, rivers, canals, and other waterways. Captains or masters are in charge of a vessel and the crew. Deck officers or mates help the captain. Seamen and deck hands do maintenance, steer, and load and unload cargo. Pilots guide ships through harbors and narrow waterways. These workers are outdoors in all kinds of weather. Many spend long periods away from home. Working on ships can be dangerous and lonely.

Something Extra

Merchant mariners working on ships on the Great Lakes typically work for 60 days straight, then have 30 days off. These long cruises involve a lot of hard work and offer little job security. Most sailors are hired for one voyage at a time. During the winter months when the lakes are frozen, there is no work at all.

So why do they do it? Most work these jobs simply because they love being on the water.

Subjects to Study

Math, physical education, swimming, first aid

Discover More

Water transportation workers must be comfortable both on and in the water. Take swimming lessons at your local park or YMCA. Then sign up for a water safety or first aid course.

Related Jobs

Fishing vessel captains, ferryboat operators, and hatch tenders

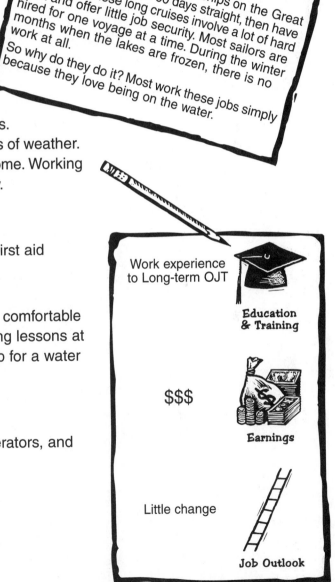

Work experience to Long-term OJT

Education & Training

$$$

Earnings

Little change

Job Outlook

Handlers,
Equipment Cleaners,
Helpers, & Laborers

Handlers, Equipment Cleaners, Helpers, & Laborers

On the Job

Handlers, equipment cleaners, helpers, and laborers do entry-level jobs, from moving boxes to cleaning work areas. They follow the directions of a supervisor and do routine tasks that help other workers work more smoothly. Many do physically demanding work, like lifting, kneeling, and crawling. Some work outdoors. Others are exposed to harmful chemicals or dangerous machinery.

Subjects to Study

Reading, basic math, physical education

Discover More

Volunteer to help out at a gas station or other small business for a day or two. You might stock shelves, sweep floors, carry boxes, or take inventory.

Related Jobs

Loggers, groundskeepers, machine operators, construction workers, assemblers, mechanics, and repairers

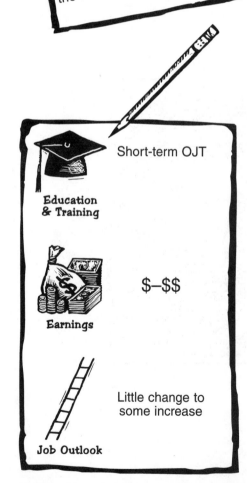

Education & Training
Short-term OJT

Earnings
$–$$

Job Outlook
Little change to some increase

Job Opportunities in the Armed Forces

Job Opportunities in the Armed Forces

Something Extra

What kind of jobs does military training prepare you for? Almost anything. The armed forces train doctors, nurses, journalists, surveyors, meteorologists, computer specialists, pilots, sailors, electronics equipment repairers, mechanics, and craft workers. Many employers like hiring former military personnel because they know about discipline, honor, and getting the job done.

On the Job

The U.S. armed forces are the country's largest employer. Maintaining a strong defense requires many activities, such as running hospitals, repairing helicopters, programming computers, and operating nuclear reactors. Military jobs range from clerical work to professional positions to construction work. People in the military must serve for a specified time and can be moved from one base to another. Many work nights, weekends, and holidays, and combat duty is always possible.

Subjects to Study

Math, English, business, sciences, shop courses, physical education

Discover More

Do you think you would enjoy military life? Talk to people who have served in the armed forces. Contact a recruiter to find out about a particular branch of the military. (Remember, though, that a recruiter's job is to get people to join.)

Related Jobs

Nearly any civilian job

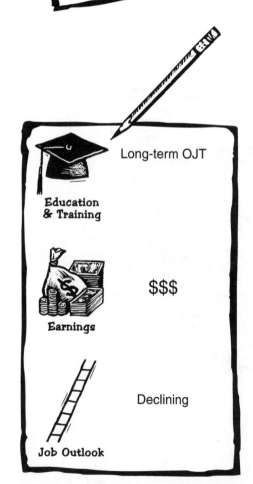

Education & Training — Long-term OJT

Earnings — $$$

Job Outlook — Declining

Job Title Index

A

Accountants & Auditors, 10
Actors, Directors, & Producers, 123
Actuaries, 56
Adjusters, Investigators, & Collectors, 140
Administrative Services Managers, 11
Adult Education Teachers, 81
Aerospace Engineers, 41
Agricultural Scientists, 62
Air Traffic Controllers, 39
Aircraft Mechanics, Including Engine Specialists, 194
Aircraft Pilots, 38
Apparel Workers, 252
Architects, 52
Archivists & Curators, 82
Armed Forces, 272
Automotive Body Repairers, 195
Automotive Mechanics, 196

B

Bank Tellers, 141
Barbers & Cosmetologists, 179
Billing Clerks & Billing Machine Operators, 159
Bindery Workers, 249
Biological & Medical Scientists, 63
Blue-Collar Worker Supervisors, 235
Boilermakers, 240
Bookkeeping, Accounting, & Auditing Clerks, 160
Bricklayers & Stonemasons, 218
Broadcast Technicians, 115
Brokerage Clerks & Statement Clerks, 161
Budget Analysts, 12
Bus Drivers, 262
Butchers & Meat, Poultry, & Fish Cutters, 238

C

Cardiovascular Technologists & Technicians, 104
Carpenters, 219
Carpet Installers, 220
Cashiers, 128
Chefs, Cooks, & Other Kitchen Workers, 172
Chemical Engineers, 42
Chemists, 65
Chiropractors, 89
Civil Engineers, 44
Clerical Supervisors & Managers, 142
Clinical Laboratory Technologists & Technicians, 105
College & University Faculty, 83
Commercial & Industrial Electronic Equipment Repairers, 199
Communications Equipment Repairers, 200
Computer & Office Machine Repairers, 201
Computer Operators, 143

Computer Programmers, 57
Computer Scientists, Computer Engineers, & Systems Analysts, 58
Concrete Masons & Terrazzo Workers, 221
Construction & Building Inspectors, 13
Construction Managers, 14
Correctional Officers, 187
Cost Estimators, 15
Counselors, 84
Counter & Rental Clerks, 129
Court Reporters, Medical Transcriptionists, & Stenographers, 144

D

Dancers & Choreographers, 124
Dental Assistants, 174
Dental Hygienists, 106
Dental Laboratory Technicians, 257
Dentists, 90
Designers, 120
Diesel Mechanics, 197
Dietitians & Nutritionists, 95
Dispatchers, 154
Dispensing Opticians, 107
Drafters, 53
Drywall Workers & Lathers, 222

E

Economists & Marketing Research Analysts, 72
Education Administrators, 16
EEG Technologists, 108
Electric Power Generating Plant Operators & Power Distributors & Dispatchers, 246
Electrical & Electronics Engineers, 44
Electricians, 223
Electronic Equipment Repairers, 198
Electronic Home Entertainment Equipment Repairers, 202
Elevator Installers & Repairers, 204
Emergency Medical Technicians, 109
Employment Interviewers, 17
Engineering Technicians, 51
Engineering, Science, & Computer Systems Managers, 18
Engineers, 40

F

Farm Equipment Mechanics, 205
Farmers & Farm Managers, 19
File Clerks, 162
Financial Managers, 20
Firefighters, 188
Fishers, Hunters, & Trappers, 236

Young Person's Electronic Occupational Outlook Handbook CD-ROM

Based on the *Young Person's Occupational Outlook Handbook,* this CD-ROM is engaging, fun, and appealing to kids. Job descriptions are accessed easily by title and by job cluster. Hundreds of color photos show people at work in the occupations being described.

Descriptions cover 85 percent of the workforce. Each entry includes the following information:

- Brief job description

- Details on working conditions

- School subjects related to the job

- Suggested activities for trying out the job

- Information on earnings, education or training needed, and employment outlook

ISBN 1-56370-619-9

$295.00 • Order Code J6199

Every occupation can be printed out on one page, so students can have a hard copy of the information. IBM/Mac versions available.

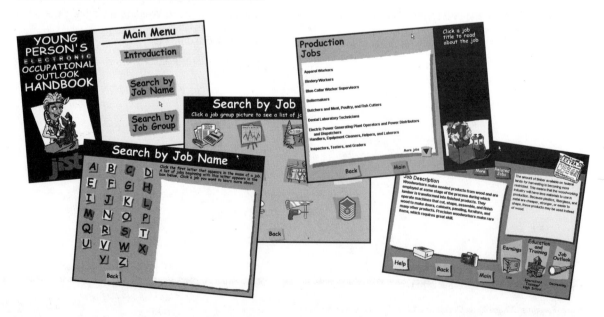